HEY THERE!
YOU WITH THE STARS IN YOUR EYES.
HAVE YOU HEARD ABOUT—

✳ How to get a 75%/25% book deal for novelizations of your screenplay—and the right to use the artwork from the movie and its title

✳ How to protect yourself if the studio buys your screenplay and sits on it . . . that is, never makes the picture

✳ Why bonuses only increase your chance of *being kicked off* a project at an early stage if the studio can find a cheaper writer

✳ What two important provisions you should negotiate and can get *if you ask for them,* when you have a percentage of profits

✳ What payments you can get if the studio produces a sequel picture or a television series based on your script . . . only *if you ask for them*

✳ What up-front guarantees you must negotiate if you are commissioned to write a screenplay—with payoffs that can *add thousands* to what you make, along with pension payments and other extras

✳ Why you must NEVER blurt out an idea at a cocktail party . . . and how to keep producers from stealing your ideas

CLAUSE BY CLAUSE
THE SCREENWRITER'S LEGAL GUIDE

QUANTITY SALES

Most Dell books are available at special quantity discounts when purchased in bulk by corporations, organizations, or groups. Special imprints, messages, and excerpts can be produced to meet your needs. For more information, write to: Dell Publishing, 1540 Broadway, New York, NY 10036. Attention: Director, Special Markets.

INDIVIDUAL SALES

Are there any Dell books you want but cannot find in your local stores? If so, you can order them directly from us. You can get any Dell book currently in print. For a complete up-to-date listing of our books and information on how to order, write to: Dell Readers Service, Box DR, 1540 Broadway, New York, NY 10036.

THE SCREENWRITER'S LEGAL GUIDE

CLAUSE BY CLAUSE

STEPHEN F. BREIMER, ESQ.

A DELL TRADE PAPERBACK

A DELL TRADE PAPERBACK

Published by
Dell Publishing
a division of
Bantam Doubleday Dell Publishing Group, Inc.
1540 Broadway
New York, New York 10036

Library of Congress Cataloging in Publication Data

Breimer, Stephen F.
    Clause by clause : the screenwriter's legal guide / Stephen F. Breimer.
       p.   cm.
    Includes index.
    ISBN 0-440-50561-5
    1. Motion picture industry—Law and legislation—United States. 2. Authors and publishers—United States. 3. Screenwriters—Legal status, laws, etc.—United States. I. Title.
KF4302.B74   1995
808.2'3—dc20   94-48672
                                     CIP

Printed in the United States of America

Published simultaneously in Canada

September 1995

10 9 8 7 6 5 4 3 2 1

BVG

For my writer clients
whom I am proud to represent.

For the screenwriters:

*Film is a collaborative medium, but without you,
there would be no opportunities for the other
collaborators.*

CONTENTS

CLAUSE
BY CLAUSE

PREFACE

How often have newcomers to Hollywood—and old-timers too—wished that they could put the expertise of a Hollywood lawyer to work for them, without the high price tag? Here is a book that explains the Hollywood vocabulary of lawyers and agents talking about the various terms of a screenwriter's contract.

As Robert Altman's 1992 movie, *The Player*, shows, a writer's life in Hollywood can be a hazardous one. (The hapless writer is murdered by his producer!) When writers gather in L.A., they often spend the entire evening regaling each other with horrendous can-you-top-this stories. The Writers Guild maintains a busy docket hearing the grievances of members who allege exploitation. And various computerized bulletin boards around town make sure that everyone knows about the latest contractual wrinkle, new level of option money or unscrupulous producer's behavior. If you are already established and on the grapevine, that is one thing. But what if you are just starting out? What if you have sold a few screenplays and suspect that you could be doing better? Or, perhaps you are a smart attorney who wants to break into this fascinating branch of show biz. Or a literary agent.

CLAUSE BY CLAUSE: THE SCREENWRITER'S LE-
GAL GUIDE is for all of you. This book will take the reader
through various types of film and television negotiations,
explaining the terminology in clear, layperson's language.
By keeping this book close at hand, you will see what is
possible, will understand industry norms and will have a
better grasp of the process.

INTRODUCTION

I am a partner in one of Los Angeles' better known entertainment law firms. We have conducted thousands of negotiations over the years—everything from a fledgling writer's first deal to a top screenwriter's negotiations with a major studio, and screen rights deals ranging from block-buster best-sellers to that tiny, precious novel. I know how important it is for the writer to understand what is being negotiated. Fewer surprises mean more satisfied clients; more satisfied clients have more successful careers.

I always make it a point to involve my clients in the negotiation of their deals. For me, it is important that my clients understand their rights and why they need to be protected. Most enjoy the process. Unfortunately, I do not have the time to review every clause of every deal with every client. I also recognize that the time involved to do that would be costly.

I have often wished that I could direct my clients to a reference book which would explain the process of negoti-ation and the meaning of the many terms that appear in sales and services agreements. There is no such book. Based on the questions which I am most commonly asked, and based on the questions which *should* be asked, I am writing this book.

Art Buchwald has shown that in the world of Hollywood, the elusive term *net profits* has often been interpreted as if seen through a funhouse mirror. Indeed, Hollywood historically has held a rather cavalier attitude toward writers' services. For these reasons alone, writers and their agents need all the knowledge they can get.

Understand that I am not advocating that you negotiate a deal all by yourself. But by using this book, together with the right professional, you will learn much about what you need to know about interpreting a contract and what to expect in the process.

Imagine now that you are a working screenwriter—one of the fortunate ones whose efforts are finally paying off. You have worked hard to create a piece of material that someone wants to acquire. Or, you have worked hard to develop your writing talent and someone wants to hire you. Negotiations have begun and, hopefully, you will be asked to sign a contract—a legal, binding contract in which the rights to your labor of love will be owned and controlled by someone else. If you have never read a writer's contract, or, even if you have, you will probably have many questions.

As negotiations continue, you will be pressured. You do not want to lose the deal. Your agent or lawyer explains the terms. All sorts of new phrases are thrown at you . . . options, representations, warranties, passive payments, obligations, bonuses for sole writing credit, sequels, this or that, and lengthy "Buchwald-type" profit definitions. You are advised that the proposal is a good one or a bad one. You are not sure. You have a hundred questions. There is no time to explain it all. You are confused. Finally, you decide to rely on your advisor's recommendations. That person knows. You do not, but it is a deal. Hopefully, as time goes on, you will become knowledgeable. For now, ignorance is not bliss, but it will do. You need the money.

I have been in your shoes. Before I was a lawyer, I produced movies. I also did some writing. In the beginning, I did not have enough money to hire a lawyer and I did not have an agent. I sometimes worked without a contract. I got burned. When I finally started demanding contracts, I asked a few questions and signed without fully understanding. I still did not have a lawyer. Luckily, it turned out all right.

Finally I retained a lawyer, a great lawyer, Peter Dekom, who is now my partner. His best advice to me at the time was to read my contracts and to *understand* them. A contract is one's guide to the level of performance expected and certain conditional bonuses. Reading a contract should not be hell, and it will not be, if you understand it. Nothing should be a secret to you. A lawyer or agent can make recommendations and great deals, but the best deals are made with the full participation of the client. You want to be able to participate in the negotiation of your contract. At the end of the day, it is *your* contract, your obligations, your money. Remember—you are signing it, not your agent or your lawyer.

You will be asked to make decisions, and you will want to make them intelligently. You should not be asked to sign something you do not understand. Inevitably, you, the writer, will be asked to sign a lengthy contract based on an agent's and/or lawyer's advice and expertise. But many questions, I am sure, will go unanswered. I understand this. Business must go on. Agreements have to be finalized quickly or deals can be lost.

You may decide to leave it to the lawyers and agents to make decisions on your behalf. The problem with that approach is not so much that the decision may be wrong for you, but that you may be *surprised*.

Many contracts have quirky provisions. Take the following example—a client of mine was astonished when he realized how this provision works: In most cases, when a writer options a script to a studio for one year, it is for one year. At one studio, however, that one year can be extended without the studio paying more to extend it. My client optioned his screenplay to a major Hollywood studio for one year and he was hired to rewrite the script. That particular studio has a policy that, for purposes of computing the one-year period, the one-year period does not *begin* until the writer turns in all of his rewrites. My client took more than the allotted time for his rewrites, with the studio's blessing. What they knew, and what he did not, was that the studio still had one year, no matter when he finished his rewrites. He had forgotten that this provision was in his contract and it came as a surprise.

Another provision many writers forget: Many contracts put you in breach for behavior that is commonplace. For example, when hiring a writer, the studio will almost always require that writing services be exclusive. One is not supposed to be working on two scripts at once or for different people. Do writers do it? Yes. Often. Do they get away with it? Sometimes, by not talking about the other project that they are writing. It is usually not a problem, but it *could* be. In fact, it can be grounds for termination. You need to know that before you decide to take the chance. I always advise my clients of the risk. I also point out that if it becomes a problem, the studio may be compassionate—as long as you can deliver your draft on time. If they are extremely compassionate, you might get more time. It depends on the circumstances and how much in favor you are. Ultimately, you will have to make the decision, but you should know that you are at risk and that by working on two scripts at once for different employers, you are in breach of your contract. For that reason I do not recommend it.

I assume that you have chosen to read this book because you *do not* want to be surprised. The other major benefit of understanding the various clauses in your contract is that you will be able to follow the negotiations and participate in the process. And you probably want to be assured that your representative is looking out for your best interests. I will never forget one particular negotiation that took place when I was a producer. In that negotiation, the lawyer on the other side, in my opinion, was *not* representing his client's best interests. The negotiation was a nightmare. The writer's lawyer had unrealistic demands and asked for extraordinary provisions. I finally closed the deal, but the negotiation left such a sour taste that I later abandoned the project. Looking back, I realize that I blamed the writer for these demands and I should not have. He was poorly represented. You want to make sure that does not happen to you.

I was asked to write this book by a good friend of mine, an extraordinary literary agent named Charlotte Sheedy. She told me there is no such book. We agreed that one is needed and I am glad that I have been given the opportunity to help. This book is your guide, if you want to (and you should) learn more about the negotiation and terms of your contract. It will also help you and your advisor to speed up the process, an essential step in the running of your own unique business.

By using this book, together with the right professional, hopefully you will learn most everything you need to know about interpreting a contract and what to expect in the process. Understand that I am not advocating that you negotiate a deal all by yourself. Your responsibility is to understand the process.

The best contracts are written in plain English. Unfortunately, they are usually not drafted that way. "Legalese" is the vocabulary and it often intimidates the reader. This book is designed to help you to understand these contracts in plain English. In it, I have delineated some of the best deals one can get. At the very least, you should understand what is possible, what essential protections you must have, what you should expect, and what is dreaming. I have found that the most successful artists in Hollywood read their agreements and participate in the negotiation of their contracts. They understand what is expected of them and what special perks they have been given. That understanding invariably helps to create a strong professional relationship.

Yours is an exciting business. With knowledge, you will find that the process of negotiation is a challenging, rewarding one. You have arrived. Someone is excited about your work. The work has value and you have some negotiating power. Remember, until you finish negotiating, your work cannot be used, duplicated or ripped off (provided it is more than an idea—a concept discussed at length later in the book). Your dreams are coming true. I want you to enjoy the process.

CHAPTER ONE

THE SCREENWRITER HOLDS A UNIQUE POSITION IN HOLLYWOOD

A. HISTORY

In order for you to understand the basic philosophy of the studios (the main buyers of writers' scripts and employers of their services), it is important to appreciate the historical position of the screenwriter in Hollywood.

Since the inception of the film *business,* studios have considered the screenwriter a disposable employee. *Hired help.* In the early days studios employed stables of writers. They were exclusive to a particular studio and the studios were thus able to commission each script using many contributors, each with his own specialty. A writer known for structure would be brought in to help if the problem was structural. If the problem was romance, a romantic writer would come on board to write a love scene. Sometimes a writer would be brought in just for one scene. *Gone With the Wind,* for example, had sixteen different writers. Famous playwrights like Ben Hecht and John Van Druten were brought in to write words and scenes. F. Scott Fitzgerald was hired to edit and reshape the structure of the screenplay. Producers like David O. Selznick (who produced *Gone With the Wind*) were the contractors, writers were the laborers.

Most writers of feature films today are hired freelance, but the philosophy is the same. Like their predecessors, writers are often replaced. New writers are often brought in for drafts, rewrites and polishes. Scripts might go through ten drafts and ten writers. *Tootsie* is one such example. Three writers were credited. Many came in just to write scenes and even lines.

The same philosophy prevails even if you sell a script. Unlike book writers or playwrights, who usually do their own rewriting and often have the last word (indeed the Dramatists Guild for playwrights *insists* that the playwright must be the only writer unless he/she consents to bring someone else in), Hollywood writers are almost always rewritten, even the best of them, even those who sell finished scripts. Virtually no script sold is *ever* the final draft, so someone will have to be hired and the buyer of an existing script (such script is commonly known as a "spec script") usually assumes the same attitude as if such script had been commissioned from the start. Often, writers of such scripts are never consulted again, and invariably they are cut out of the process of making movies. This reality constantly reinforces the attitude that writers are hired help.

Of course, if you sell a spec script, you will try to ensure that you are hired for at least one rewrite and maybe more. This all depends on leverage and how "hot" the screenplay is *(hot* meaning that there is more than one buyer out there when it is sent out).

But, in short, no matter how good the deal is, just as

in the days of the old Hollywood, once the deal is made, most writers accept the fact that they will have to walk away from their material.

B. A WORK MADE FOR HIRE

The attitude toward writers derives in part from the fact that Hollywood is a *business*. When studios and producers pay writers to write, they own the material. The notion that the writer is an artist, while recognized, has little or no bearing on the writer's legal relationship to his/her work.

Under the 1976 Copyright Act, a "commissioned work," meaning that the writer is paid to write something (as distinguished from being paid for an already existing piece of material such as a spec script), is called a "work made for hire." A work made for hire is, specifically, material prepared within the scope of an employment relationship or "work specially ordered or commissioned for use as a contribution to a collective work, as part of a motion picture or other audiovisual work." (17 U.S.C.§ 101 [1976].) You will actually see this language in your employment agreements. All writing assignments are works made for hire. And what that means essentially is that the written material belongs to the studio or employer, because under the Copyright Act, by paying for it to be written, the employer *owns* the material. "In the case of a work made for hire, the employer or other person for whom the work was prepared is considered the author for purposes of this title, and, unless the parties have expressly agreed otherwise in a written instrument signed by them, owns all of the rights comprised in the copyright." (17 U.S.C.§ 201

[1976].) Here is a sample "work for hire" provision from a studio contract:

> *Results and Proceeds.* Artist acknowledges that all of the results and proceeds of Artist's services hereunder are and will be created by Artist as a "work-made-for-hire" *and/or a work* specially ordered or commissioned by Studio *for use as a part of a contribution to a collective work, as part of a motion picture or other audiovisual work, with Studio being deemed the sole author of all such results and proceeds.* Artist acknowledges that Studio is and shall be the sole and exclusive owner of all rights of every kind and nature in, to and with respect to Artist's services hereunder and the results and proceeds thereof and that Studio shall have the right to use, refrain from using, change, modify, add to, subtract from and to exploit, advertise, exhibit and otherwise turn to account any or all of the foregoing in any manner and in any and all media (including, without limitation, in and in connection with theatrical and nontheatrical motion pictures [including, without limitation, *remakes and sequels]*, all forms of television, radio, legitimate stage, videodiscs, videocassettes and all other home video devices, phonograph recordings, publications and merchandising), whether now known or hereafter devised, throughout the world, in perpetuity, in all languages, as Studio in its sole discretion shall determine.

Since the studio owns all material from the start, the studio believes in the philosophy that the studio can do anything they want with it, subject, of course, to the terms of the writer's contract. While I have many problems with the prevalent Hollywood attitude toward writers as disposable manpower, I cannot in good conscience put all the blame on the Hollywood financiers. We must go farther back in history. The choice of words contained in our copyright law emphasizes the disposable role of the writer. The employer is not treated *as if it is* the author, but *is considered* the author. This language certainly did not help writers! By treating the employers—the studios—as *authors,* our own laws have helped to reinforce the philosophy that the employed writer can be forgotten. He is not even the *author* of his own work. The choice of words was, to say the least, unfortunate. Designed to give the employer the same ownership rights that the non-employee writer has, it does more. By adding credence to the mentality that an employed writer is just a hired hand, it takes away much of the respect that he may have had as an author and serves to justify the studio attitude.

C. FILM IS A DIRECTOR'S MEDIUM

The other factor which contributes to the placement of writers at the bottom of the Hollywood hierarchy is the utmost respect given to directors. You have probably heard the expression that film is a "director's medium." The notion that directors are the stars (aside from the cast) is a fact which is clearly validated and promoted by the studios.

For one, star directors tend to be paid much more than star writers and star producers. The minimum for a star director today would be $1,500,000–$2,000,000, and that is low. I have a director client who was just offered $6,000,000 for his next film. No writer has ever been paid that much.

In addition, directors customarily receive profits in the form of "adjusted gross," as compared to the writer's "net profits." "Adjusted gross" is much better. Indeed, there is a major financial difference between adjusted gross and net profits (see discussion in Chapter Three I).

That is not to say writers never receive adjusted gross, but it is extremely rare and some studios categorically refuse to give writers adjusted gross, even if the writer's last script was turned into a movie that generated more than $100,000,000 at the box office. The studio prefers to reward a successful writer in other ways, so as not to destroy the precedent in Hollywood that star writers are lower on the totem pole than star actors and directors. For example, the studio may also hire a successful writer as a "producer" (in name) and give that writer a piece of adjusted gross for his so-called services as a "producer." This is a clever solution—primarily designed to deal with the precedent problem.

Always keep in mind that the director is considered the visionary in Hollywood, the person whom the studio is ultimately banking on to shoot the film, cut it, and complete it. While it is true that directors are replaced, the studio attitude at the onset is that the director will be on the picture until delivery of the director's cut. If anyone is going to be replaced, given a disagreement between director and writer, invariably it will be the writer. It is built into the system, and as long as a particular director is on the project, the studio will bow to the director's wishes when it comes to the choice of which writer stays or goes.

When a director is replaced, however, it sometimes helps the original writer of a screenplay. During the process of developing a screenplay, directors come on board and sometimes they are replaced during the development process. Many a director has been unable to "lick" a script —take it to the point where he/she feels comfortable directing it, notwithstanding his/her desire initially to get involved with the project. A new director may very well choose to go back to the original screenwriter. *The Verdict* was one such example. David Mamet was the original writer. Robert Redford at one time was set to star, James Bridges to direct. They chose a different writer, then abandoned the project. When Sidney Lumet came on board, he went back to Mamet's original screenplay. *WarGames* had a similar history. The writers of these screenplays were lucky survivors of the system.

As you read this book, you will undoubtedly come across customary provisions for writers that may seem outrageous. You will say, "How can they do that!?" Always remember the historical place of the screenwriter in Hollywood. It will help you to understand what might otherwise seem illogical or unfair. It also helps to remember that the film industry is a big business. As films get more and more expensive to make, we need the conglomerate media companies to continue financing them. In short, do not bite the hand that feeds you. Understand the system, accept it, and you can be a success. Whine about it and you will be labeled as a whiner. It is not an attractive posture. Of course, changes can and will be made within the system. But the system is the system. It is unlikely to change. And your negotiations should be about getting the best there is to offer within that system and not to change it.

CHAPTER TWO

CONTRACTS:
A BRIEF OVERVIEW

The working writer needs to be knowledgeable about two kinds of contracts—"employment agreements" (when you are hired) and "literary acquisition" or "option" agreements (when you grant someone else the rights to one of your existing works). Of course, many screenwriter agreements may combine the two, but for the moment, I want to make sure you understand the particulars of each type of agreement. Then we will examine the combination agreements. Remember always that negotiation of these agreements is about leverage, and leverage for the screenwriter, even the best, is limited by the attitude which I have discussed in Chapter One.

If you are a Writers Guild member, you will be entitled to certain valuable protections accorded by the Writers Guild Basic Agreement (sometimes referred to as the "MBA," the "Minimum Basic Agreement," or the "WGA Agreement"). Many of the provisions which I discuss in this book are automatically given to you because you are a member. However, the Guild protections are minimum protections and writers are often able to obtain better terms by negotiation and by contract. If you are a beginning writer, you will have the most leverage when someone approaches you about a script that you have written. Remember, you do not *have* to sell it unless you are comfortable with the deal. The same holds true for seasoned writers. If they have something that someone else wants, they will get the best deal. If not, they may have to take what is offered.

I am going to start with an outline of an option/purchase agreement (a contract dealing with the option or sale of existing literary material). By understanding the best of these deals (those obtained with the most leverage), you will understand what is theoretically possible under the best of circumstances, and by understanding that, you will understand the variables involved in the sale or acquisition of material.

As mentioned in Chapter One, an existing script which is sold or optioned (not a "work made for hire") is called a "spec script." That is because the writer has written it with only a speculation that someone might buy it. Several years ago buying spec scripts was the rage. At that time, studios sometimes paid $1,000,000 for what they thought was a hot property. *The Last Boy Scout* is one such example. In that instance, studios bid against each other and the writer of that screenplay was able to walk away with over $1,000,000 in cash and a promising deal. *Black Rain* was another such example. I represented the writer of that script and it was very exciting. We closed the deal very quickly. Such a sale is a writer's dream.

The spec script market today is limited, although lately it seems to be picking up again. Studios realized that a huge outlay of cash did not necessarily ensure a hit, and today the studios are all on a budget kick. The recession also put a lot of independent companies out of business. With the majority of Hollywood's spending dollars in the hands of the studios, they were basically able, once they decided to pull back, to limit the spec market. That is not to say that scripts are not purchased outright, but the instances today are fewer than before, so do not count on it. And remember, there is a lot of competition. Agents, readers and executives spend mornings, evenings and weekends reading and poring over new submissions.

To put this business in perspective for you, an agent friend of mine at a large major agency told me that he had spent the weekend with his favorite relative. He had not seen her in a long time and he wanted to carve out as much time as possible over the weekend to spend with her. She was old. He also had to deal with his normal workload. "I obviously couldn't get all my weekend work done," he said to me, "but I did spend ten hours reading." I said, "You must have read a lot of scripts." "Scripts?" he asked. "I spent ten hours reading *coverage.*" *Coverage* in Hollywood terms is a reader's short summary of a screenplay (usually a couple of pages) with a recommendation at the end: Read, Pass, Consider. Ten hours spent reading coverage means coverage of at least two hundred scripts, probably more. In short, there is a lot out there and a lot of material. If someone wants to *buy* your script, consider yourself lucky. All in all, the percentage of spec script sales to the number of screenplays offered for sale in a given year is very low.

More likely, if you have written a spec script, it will be optioned. The next chapter explains in detail the basic provisions of what is commonly called the "Option/Purchase Agreement."

CHAPTER THREE

OPTION/PURCHASE AGREEMENTS: NEGOTIATING FOR AN EXISTING WORK (SPEC SCRIPTS AND BOOKS)

Now I want you to sit back, relax and pretend that your agent and lawyer are about to begin discussions. The main concept to grasp is that your script is an asset—a bundle of various rights. Naturally, the buyer's goal is to obtain as many of those rights as he can get, for as little money as possible.

Because of the competition and the reluctance to spend huge sums of money, studios and producers usually take an option on spec scripts. The option literally gives the buyer the option to purchase the material at a later date for a specific price. This agreement is called an "option/purchase agreement."

A. OPTIONS

1. Price

The option price is the price the producer pays to gain exclusive control of a certain piece of material. That option will be for a certain period of time, at the end of which time the producer must "exercise" his option (acquire the rights—see discussion below in Chapter Three F). or lose his right to buy rights in that material. The price paid for the material is usually called the "purchase price." The option agreement stipulates certain requirements for exercise of the option. Usually there is a requirement of notice to the owner and payment of a set purchase price established at the time the option/purchase agreement is negotiated. Note that the purchase price is generally paid at the time of exercise (the end of the option period) but sometimes the purchase price is paid at other times. (See discussion in Chapter Three D.)

Options can be any length. The standard option is for one year, and often there are renewal or extension periods. It takes a long time to get a movie made. Studios want the time to develop the script and to bring the right director and stars on board. Thus, they will insist on at least one additional year and sometimes more.

Option prices are very small in comparison to the purchase price. There is no rule. A standard option payment for a feature film from a major studio is $10,000–$25,000 for one year—sometimes more, sometimes less.

You should be aware that studio producers also receive very little money during the development period. Contrary to what you might think, they usually receive less money than the writer during this period. While it is true that many producers of studio pictures receive high salaries if a picture gets made, they do not get these salaries if the project does not get made. The customary studio producer development fee (the producer's salary during the development stage before the picture is shot) is $25,000. This salary is paid only when the project is set up with a financier *and* the first writer begins to render services. If the first writer to be hired cannot start working for six months, the producer does not get paid for six months. One half of the development fee is payable on commencement of the writer's services and one half when the studio decides either to abandon the project or to produce it. Remember, producers have to live on that money until a project is "greenlighted" (the Hollywood expression for the point in time when the studio decides to finance the movie). This could be many years away. In short, until the studio decides to make a project, you and the producer are in the same boat. The option is going to be low and their salary is low. But you, unlike the producer, will probably receive some sort of writing fee on top of the option payment. (See discussion below in Chapter Four.)

When an independent producer options a script, he or she usually pays a much lower option fee than the studio—customarily $2,500–$5,000 for one year. The independent producer's argument, and it is a fair one, is that his/her most valuable contribution is the effort to get the studio interested in the project and to get the picture made. If you agree to give an independent producer an option for little money, however, you should protect yourself with what is called a "setup bonus." Your best argument when dealing with an independent producer who will only give you a low option fee is to say, "Okay, if I accept your low offer and I believe you will get the picture made, then I want another payment when you do set it up at a studio. Say another $10,000.'' This is quite customary. Studios will accept it and you should insist on it. You will be paid your setup bonus when the producer sets the project up at the studio. Legally, this may be when he makes the deal with the studio or, more commonly, when he *signs* the deal with the studio. This is negotiable. Each studio has its own policy in that regard.

Another main area of bargaining with respect to option payments is whether the option payment is applicable against the purchase price or not. Thus, for example, if the option price for the first year is $5,000, the purchase price for the script is $200,000, and the $5,000 option payment is applicable against the purchase price, you would receive $195,000 at the time of purchase. Generally, the first option payment for the first option period is applicable. Subsequent payments are not. Of course, it is all negotiable. The setup bonus may also be applicable or non-applicable. The payment of the setup bonus might also extend the option.

Example: The producer has a one-year option for $5,000, renewable for a second year for $5,000 and renewable again for a third year for $10,000. (Keep in mind that the longer the producer wants to hold on to the material, the better your position is to raise the option payment in the later option years.) The purchase price is $200,000. The first option payment is applicable against the purchase price; the second and third payments are not applicable against the purchase price. There is a setup bonus of $10,000 which extends the option for another year past the setup date (the date on which you are to receive the setup bonus), but the setup bonus is not applicable against the purchase price. Let us say the option begins on January 1,

1993, and the producer sets up the project on June 6, 1993. You will receive $5,000 on January 1, 1993. You will receive $10,000 on June 6, 1993. The initial option period would have expired on December 31, 1993, if it had not been set up. With the setup fee extension, the first option period expires on June 5, 1994. The option may be extended two more times per the contract. You will receive another $5,000 on June 6, 1994, and $10,000 on June 6, 1995. The option expires on June 5, 1996. If the script is purchased, how much will you receive? Since the only applicable payment is the first one, you will receive $195,000 at the time of purchase. You will have received in this example a total of $5,000 (first option payment) + $10,000 (setup bonus) + $5,000 (second option payment) + $10,000 (third option payment) + $195,000 (purchase price) for a total of $225,000.

Sometimes producers look for a free option. The general attitude about this is that if the producer is really committed, the producer should put his/her money where his/her mouth is. Something, at least.

I have found, generally, that producers who ask for a free option do not get the picture made any faster than those who pay. Producers are generally juggling many projects. They have to. And just because it is free does not mean they will give it any more attention. In fact, they may give it less attention because they have not spent any money on it (other than legal fees, of course, to draft the option, which, depending on the length of the negotiation, may be costly).

My attitude is that you probably should not give anyone a free ride, unless the producer has a tremendous track record, is a good friend, or you have no other offers. The option is worth something. You are taking the script *off* the market for the option period (and it will probably be shown and *covered* everywhere, possibly destroying its future value). No other producer can touch it. Producers are in business—remember, it is a business—and they should treat the transaction that way. They will buy a refrigerator for their house—they should pay for your material. Also keep in mind that if you use a lawyer, you will be out of pocket unless you use a percentage lawyer—a lawyer who receives a percentage of what you receive. If you do not use a percentage lawyer, it will cost you money to negotiate the deal at the time you negotiate it.

Television options are usually much lower than feature options and there is a reason. Producers who option projects for television, and features for that matter, generally expect the network or studio to reimburse them for option payments when they set up the project at the network or studio, as applicable. The networks keep option reimbursement payments low, $1,500–$2,500 for six months to one year. Studios, on the other hand, will generally reimburse the full cost of an option for a feature, within reason, and do not impose artificial ceilings. If the producer of a television project has already paid you a $5,000 option—the networks do not care. The producer eats it. That does not mean you cannot fight for a higher price. Try. Producers of TV movies (more specifically, "supplier producers" who own the right to exploit their movies after the initial network order, which is generally two runs) earn a lot if the picture is made, sometimes up to $750,000–$1,000,000 if you include all sales of the picture over the years. They can earn that much because the networks have until recently been prohibited (unlike the studios for features) from owning most of the product they put on the air (see Chapter Four E.1). The general rule, however, is that most producers will not go out of pocket, and if they do, option prices in TV are rarely over $5,000.

2. Time

Your other major bargaining point in respect of options is time. If the producer is going to pay you only $1,500, then make it a short option (six months instead of the customary one-year period), with possible renewals for additional money. That is enough time for a producer to cover the networks and/or the studios and to find out if there is any interest. If they cannot set it up in six months, then you should get your project back.

B. NON-NEGOTIATED OPTION EXTENSIONS

Most option contracts give the purchaser the right to extend the option under certain unusual circumstances for no additional compensation.

1. Force Majeure Events

The option may be extended for a "force majeure event." A force majeure event is usually defined as: "an act of God, war, a labor strike which affects (shuts down) the motion picture, television and theatrical industry." More specifically, a force majeure event is an event beyond the studio's control, such as a writer's strike (even though arguably such an event is within the control of the studio— i.e., if the studio would only give in to the applicable demands, there would not be a strike. Studios, of course, do not look at it that way!). From the studio's perspective, if there's a writer's strike, the studio cannot develop your script. So they get an automatic extension.

Your representative should try to make sure that the contract stipulates that the force majeure event has to be one that directly affects the development of your project. A hurricane in Florida is a force majeure event, but if it does not affect your project, why should they get an extension?

You can also ask for a limit on the amount of time for such extensions. Some studios will agree to six months (in some cases, one year) in the aggregate for any and all force majeure extensions during the option period.

Your representative should also ensure that, even though such extensions are automatic, the studio will notify you in writing of the extension, so that you can keep track of the option period.

2. Claims

Studio contracts also provide that if there is a claim made against your script, the studio gets an extension. Suppose another writer claims that you have stolen his material? Suppose someone else claims that they have rights in your script? Studios usually will not give a ceiling on these extensions. Claims such as these put the whole project in jeopardy. They are treated very seriously.

In fact, there is a standard clause which states that if there is a claim, you will have to repay all the money you have received. Generally, I am able to get this provision deleted. The studio always has the right to prove that you did steal someone's material, and if you did, then you will have to pay damages. The concept of automatic repayment is an insulting one. There may be several bad eggs in Hollywood, but the presumption should not be that you have stolen someone else's material just because someone has made a claim. In a highly visible and lucrative business, there will always be people making claims to see if they can get something out of it. These are called "nuisance suits."

C. SHOPPING BEHIND YOUR BACK

Unfortunately, there exist producers who may express interest in a script, drag out the negotiations and, in the meantime, shop your script to the major buyers (i.e., the studios). If all the studios pass, the negotiations fall apart and you are left with a script that can become worthless.

As I mentioned above, scripts are "covered," particularly by the buyers. A reader reads the script and makes a recommendation. If it is a pass, the whole episode is recorded in the studio's ledger. If the script is resubmitted, the studio simply looks at its records and gives the same response. Some writers change the name of the project or their names when resubmitting a script. It usually does not work. Records are such that someone at the studio will probably be able to find or remember the coverage of the earlier submission before the script is actually read by an executive, so do not count on this route to get a second chance. Once it is a pass, most studios will not relook at a project unless the project is resubmitted with a major "element" (star or director) attached.

The Writers Guild recently added a provision prohibiting the submission of scripts without an option/purchase agreement in place or without specific permission. Article 49 of the Guild Agreement provides:

A. TELEVISION

Company may not shop literary material to a third party or parties without first obtaining in a separate written document the writer's consent that the literary material may be shopped to the designated third party or parties.

B. THEATRICAL

The Company may not shop literary material to a third party or parties if the writer requests, in writing, that the material not be shopped. If the writer requests, in writing, that the script be shopped only to designated third parties, Company will not shop to any other third party.

C. If the Company shops any literary material to any third party or parties in violation of the above provisions, it shall pay to the Guild for the benefit of the writer involved the sum of seven hundred fifty dollars ($750.00) for each person or company to whom the literary material has been shopped in violation of the above provisions.

Shopping is defined to mean submitting the literary material to a third party or parties and specifically does not include submitting the material to individuals within the Company. If the Company has an option to acquire motion picture or television rights in literary material, or has acquired motion picture or television rights in literary material, the Company may submit such literary material to any third party or parties without restriction or penalty, except as may be otherwise provided in the agreement granting such option or rights.

As a result of this provision, to a certain extent this behavior has been arrested, but most writers do not want to take on the producer—even if the project has been shopped—for fear that the producer will close doors for their other projects. It is a reality, alas, and relationships are important. The old saying "don't burn your bridges" is very pertinent in Hollywood. With fewer buyers nowadays, writers are often unwilling to take on major producers and it is a factor that must be considered.

D. PURCHASE OF SCREENPLAYS

1. Copyright Rights

If you have written a screenplay (other than as an employee for hire or commissioned basis), you hold the copyright in that screenplay. (See discussion in Chapter Five.) The most important point to keep in mind is that your screenplay, by virtue of your copyright, is comprised of many rights. The Copyright Act of 1976 provides the copyright holder with five different categories of exclusive rights in a copyrighted work. These are the rights of reproduction, adaptation, public distribution, public performance, and public display. (17 U.S.C.§ 106 [1976].)

The reproduction right allows the copyright holder (or his licensee—the person or entity to whom the copyright owner has licensed or sold his rights) to make copies. The adaptation right allows the holder to prepare a new or derivative work based on the copyrighted work, such as a motion picture based on a play, a new screenplay based on an existing screenplay, a sequel motion picture, TV series, etc. The public distribution right allows a work to be sold or rented, such as a book or a videocassette. The performance right allows the copyright holder to have performed his/her work publicly, such as a play or the screening of a motion picture for an audience. The right to display the copyrighted work publicly would apply to the individual frames of a motion picture, such as a still photograph. The photograph is not being performed—yet it would still be entitled to copyright protection as a display.

You should also keep in mind that a copyright is divisible under the copyright law. Not only can it be broken down into the rights as noted above, but also by medium. Thus, you can convey motion picture rights in your screenplay and the copyright in the motion picture rights and retain live stage rights and the copyright therein. Or you can convey television rights and retain publishing rights. There are numerous commutations and permutations.

This concept is a newer addition to copyright law. The older Copyright Act of 1909 talked about a single copyright (17 U.S.C.§ 10 [1909 Act]) which belonged to the author of a work and there was a single copyright proprietor. While different rights could be *licensed* to different parties (not granted to different parties, as they are today), there were certain limitations, particularly with respect to the inability to sue for copyright infringement, which right belonged only to the original copyright proprietor or someone to whom the copyright proprietor had assigned all his rights (M. Nimmer, *Nimmer on Copyright*, §10.01 [A], Volume 3, 1992). Indeed, the right to sue for infringement is one of the most important rights to be conveyed. Today a motion picture studio must have the right to sue in its name for infringement of its motion picture. A motion picture is a valuable asset (now costing sometimes in excess of $50,000,000), and it must be protected.

Under the current Copyright Act of 1976, the previous doctrine that copyright is indivisible has largely been abolished. Section 201(d)(2) of the Copyright Act is an explicit statutory recognition of the principle of divisibility of copyright. (Hou. Rep., p. 173. *National Broadcasting Co. Inc. v. Copyright Royalty Tribunal,* 848 F 2d 1289, 1295–96 [D.C. Cir. 1988].) "Any of the exclusive rights comprised in a copyright, including *any* subdivision of any of the rights specified in Section 106, may be transferred . . . and owned separately. The owner of any particular exclusive right is entitled, to the extent of that right, to all of the protection and remedies accorded to the copyright owner by this title." (17 U.S.C.§ 201(d)(2) [1976].) The term *transfer* is interpreted broadly. Thus, a hardcover tradebook edition can have its own copyright and such right could be limited to a particular time and geographic location. (M. Nimmer, *Nimmer on Copyright,* 10.02 [A], Volume 3, 1992.)

2. Rights Generally Granted

The rights you sell are the rights *granted.* The rights you retain are the *reserved* rights. Your ability to hold on to rights and to reserve them is a part of the negotiation process. That ability is always limited. Producers—and particularly studios—like to have all rights, exclusively. Very rarely is a deal made for a one-picture license. Many successful motion pictures have generated sequels *(Die Hard, Lethal Weapon).* Many have actually been developed into franchises *(Friday the 13th, Nightmare on Elm Street).* Thus, inevitably, sequel rights must be given away. The studio's argument is that it invests large sums to launch the first picture. They want the right to participate in other productions. Remake rights are treated the same way. Their argument is logical, but keep in mind that you are also entitled to additional compensation for these uses. That is the subject of a different chapter. (See Chapter Three L below.)

For now, I want you to understand the studio mentality and the essential rights you must convey in any studio deal.

To help you understand these essential rights, it is useful to read the granted rights section of any long-form studio contract. Here is an example:

The rights (granted) shall include, without limitation, the following rights:

(1) The right to produce motion pictures or other productions based upon or adapted from all or any part of the screenplay.

(2) The right to produce sound records. *[The studio always wants the ability to make money from a tie-in sound recording.]*

(3) The right to adapt, use, dramatize, arrange, change, vary, modify, alter the screenplay and any parts thereof; to add to, subtract from or omit from the screenplay, characters, language, plot, theme, scenes, incidents, situations, action, titles, dialogue, songs, music and lyrics *[this right to make changes is of essence to the screenplay contract—derived from the prevailing attitude about screenwriters as discussed above]*, to include in motion pictures, sound records and other items, such language, speech, song music, lyrics, plot, sound, sound effects, action, situations, scenes, plot dialogue, incidents and characters, characterization and other material as *Purchaser* in *its uncontrolled discretion may deem advisable; it being the intention hereof that Purchaser shall have the exclusive, absolute and unlimited right to use the screenplay and each and every part thereof for motion picture purposes in any manner it may, in its uncontrolled discretion, deem advisable with the same force and effect as though Purchaser were the sole author of the screenplay,*

specifically including, without limitation, the right to produce motion pictures as sequels, series, serials or otherwise. *[As you can see, the studios do not mince words—they want it all.]*

(4) The right to broadcast the screenplay by radio and television or otherwise.

(5) The right for the purpose of advertising and exploiting motion pictures produced hereunder, to produce and publish stories, synopses, excerpts, summaries, fictionalizations and novelizations.

(6) The right to write and prepare screenplays, teleplays, treatments, storyboards and musical compositions.

(7) The right to manufacture, sell, distribute products, by-products, services, facilities, merchandise and commodities of any nature and description, including, but not limited to, still photographs, drawings, posters, artwork, toys, games, items of wearing apparel, foods, beverages and similar items which make referral to or are based on the screenplay or any part thereof and the right to make trade deals and commercial tie-ups of all kinds. *[Again, the studio wants to be able to exploit the picture and recoup its substantial investment in many ways.* Batman, *for instance, generated millions in merchandising sales.]*

(8) The right to copyright motion pictures, sound records, musical composition, screenplays, teleplays and all other items contained in the rights granted section, together with the right to manufacture copies thereof and to distribute, sell, vend, lease, license, exhibit, transmit, broadcast, project, reproduce, publish, use, perform, advertise, publicize, market, exploit, turn to account and derive revenue in any form or manner therefrom, without any territorial restriction whatsoever by any and all means, methods, systems and processes now or hereafter known.

(9) The right to use the title by which the screenplay is now known and the right to use any other title as producer may deem proper in its uncontrolled discretion.

(10) All rights of every kind and character whatsoever other than those rights specifically reserved to owner. *[The catchall almost always goes to the buyer. The buyer wants you to spell out exactly what you are reserving. Simply put, the studio wants to know that if something is left out, they get it, not you.]*

3. Reserved Rights

The rights which are typically reserved by the writer of a spec screenplay or book (if you are hired to write, there are usually no reserved rights) are stage rights, live television rights (a holdback from the 1950s—there is virtually no live television today, but it is still a common reserved right) and radio rights.

Some screenwriters are able to reserve novelization rights, and as you will see in the discussion below, even if they are not reserved, the writer may end up with these rights anyway. Of course, the author of a book always reserves publishing rights. Some screenwriters are also able to reserve the right to publish their own screenplay. Generally, the studio will allow this only if the screenwriter is the only writer on the project. The reason: The movie may be very different than the writer's spec script. If the movie fails, the studio does not want to be embarrassed by having some critic point out that the original screenplay was better. I was recently involved in a negotiation concerning this issue, and believe it or not, the studio actually articulated the reason!

Book authors also reserve the right to create what are

called author-written sequels, i.e., a sequel or prequel book (a prequel consists of events that took place before the events in the book that is being sold). The studio, in this case, usually retains a right of first negotiation/last refusal to buy the motion picture rights to such sequels. (See subchapter 6 below.)

Here is an example of a typical reserved rights provision:

RESERVED RIGHTS: The following rights are reserved to Owner, including the copyright therein, exclusively for Owner's use and disposition, subject, however, to the provisions of this agreement:

(a) Publication Rights: The right to publish and distribute printed versions of the Work owned or controlled by Owner in book and play form, including photonovels, comic books, microfilm, microfiche, computer database, whether hardcover or softcover, and in magazines or other periodicals, whether in installments or otherwise (subject to Purchaser's 7,500-word publication rights and ten [10] minute excerpt rights provided for in paragraph 2 hereof, for advertising and promotional purposes). Such publications by Owner may be copyrighted in the name of Owner.

In no event, however, shall such publisher have the right to use the title of a motion picture produced hereunder (if different from the title heretofore used for publications of the Work) or any still photographs, artwork, trademarks, logos, or substantial literary material owned or controlled by Purchaser without Owner negotiating for said rights and Purchaser's specific written approval, which such approval shall not be unreasonably withheld.

(b) Radio rights (subject to advertising and promotion rights granted to Purchaser);

(c) Live television (subject to advertising and promotion rights);

(d) Legitimate dramatic stage rights, including cast album rights and merchandising rights in connection with such stage productions only, provided nothing contained herein shall in any way limit Purchaser's album or soundtrack rights and/or merchandising rights in connection with the Rights granted hereunder and Owner shall not be entitled to use any of Purchaser's material with respect to said rights;

The stage rights reserved by Owner hereunder do not include (and Owner shall not have) the right to authorize or permit the transmission or projection, dramatization or adaptation of the Work by means of television, disc, cartridge, cassette, computer, satellite or any process analogous thereto for the purpose of exhibition or reproduction at any theater or place of public assembly, or for exhibition or reproduction in private homes, theaters or elsewhere where any viewing fee or charge is imposed or collected as consideration from the persons observing such transmission or projection, whether paid directly or indirectly by means of cash, tokens, credit or any other manner now known or hereafter devised;

(e) All rights in Owner-written sequels (includes prequels). All references in this subparagraph to "Owner" shall be deemed to include any author of an Owner-written sequel who writes such material under authority of Owner or Owner's successor in interest.

4. Novelization and Publication Rights

It was common in the 1970s for studios to market novelizations of their movies. Writers fought to retain novelization rights and, depending on their leverage and also their ability to write a novelization, often won what was considered in those days a valuable right. Today, the novelization market is practically dead, but again, tradition allows certain writers to reserve this right.

Even if you are not successful in reserving novelization rights, if you are a member of the Writers Guild, under certain conditions you are automatically given the first opportunity to go out and find a book deal based on your screenplay. This right is yours, even if you are *commissioned* to write the screenplay. The main condition is that you must have *created* the material that is turned into a movie, and that the actual screenplay for the picture cannot be so different from your original material as to have a substantially different plot or different characters (under the WGA Agreement, this essentially means that you are entitled to "separated rights"). If you meet the criteria, you are then given a window of time in which to find a book deal. That window is very short—30 days after the studio notifies you that they want to make such a deal. However, if you are successful in obtaining a novelization deal within this time period, you are allowed to retain the major share of the book revenues—they are split 75%/25% in your favor. If you are unsuccessful, then the Guild still protects your interests. If the studio makes a novelization deal, the book revenues are shared 65%/35% in the studio's favor and you are accorded a $3,500 advance against your share. What is important is that under this arrangement, you will receive a separate payment for these rights. The revenues are not part of the net profit definition, which, as you will see below, is probably meaningless.

I generally try to improve these numbers as follows: If you make the book deal and write the book, 75%/25% in your favor. If you make the deal but do not write the book, 50%/50%. If the studio makes the deal and you write the book, 65%/35% in *your* favor. If the studio makes the deal but you do not write the book, 50%/50%. I also try to improve on the time period allowed to the writer to make a deal. Instead of 30 days, I ask for 60 to 90 days.

Even if you are not a member of the Writers Guild, you can still ask for the same provisions. In fact, generally I try to have the producer treat my non-Guild clients as if they are members of the Guild. That way, all of the benefits of the Writers Guild Basic Agreement, including provisions such as these and payment of residuals and other perks, can be integrated into your deal.

If you are successful in reserving the novelization or other publishing rights, you must make sure that you obtain the right to use the artwork from the movie and the title of the movie, if it is different from your original title. In other words, you should be able to duplicate the ads and poster logos so that the tie-in with the movie is clear. Basically, a novelization is a promotional tie-in, just like a T-shirt or soundtrack album. And that is why the studio argues that it is entitled to a share of the proceeds for the use of the artwork title and logo of the movie and usually gets it.

Sometimes you can even obtain the right to publish stills from the movie in the novelization. This is sometimes a sticky point and studios are reluctant to give it away, even when they are getting a share. If you are stuck on this latter point, pass on this one, in favor of getting the right to use the logo, artwork and title. You must have those.

When you are selling a book that you have written, of course you must insist on reserving all publication rights, including the right to continue to sell your book and the right to write novelizations or any other publication. You do not want any competing books in the marketplace that could affect or diminish the sale of your already existing book. In fact, novelization rights, including the right to use new screenplay material and the film's title and logo, should be yours for free. Assuming your book has been published, it is *you* who established a recognition of the material in the book world. Since the studio is interested in your material based on your success in that medium, you should reap all the rewards of *that medium*. The right to use the title and logo for free is sometimes hard to get, but it is worth trying for. Studios do recognize the merits of the argument that they should not share in the proceeds of a book if they have purchased a successful book to begin with, but more often than not they want their piece, too, based on the added value that a motion picture will bring to the book. Their argument is not without merit.

If you have written a book, you also want to protect all other forms of publication rights, such as photonovels, comic books, microfilm and microfiche rights and computer data base rights, including CD ROM rights. CD ROM is a new form of interactive media which is being introduced in libraries and schools. Eventually you will be able to plug into an elaborate information system through your own computer. Suppose you have written a nonfiction book about a political figure. You enter that person's name into the computer and you are able to retrieve many of the articles and books written about that person, including actual text quotes. You will want your book to be part of that system. Note that if your book is actually made into a movie, even if you do reserve CD ROM rights, the studio will not allow you to use portions of the movie in your CD ROM. Invariably, you will have to negotiate with the studio to obtain such rights and, of course, the studio will want its share.

Finally, if you are selling a book, you will want to reserve the rights for books on tape. This arena has emerged as a viable marketplace. I always ask to spell out these rights separately. It is a hybrid form of media combining audio rights and publication, but it does not really fit exactly under either category.

If you are at an impasse with the studio concerning reserved rights, then there is another alternative: to "freeze" certain rights. That means that the studio cannot do anything without you. You cannot do anything without them. That is what "frozen rights" are. You and the studio will negotiate a deal if there is interest in pursuing the exploitation of these rights at a later date. Since the primary goal is to get a movie made, there is logic in the argument that you can worry about these rights at a later time.

No matter how strong your bargaining power is, the one thing you must give the studio if you are successful in reserving publication rights is the ability to publish excerpts of your material for advertising and promotional purposes. This is important. The advertising and marketing departments need some flexibility and the right to quote different passages from your work. Generally, 7,500-word excerpt rights are acceptable, although now the trend is toward 10,000 words. Of course, if your material is only a short story, the excerpt rights should be considerably less. In that case, you might limit the excerpt privilege to a percentage of the total work—say 5%–10%.

5. Merchandising Rights

Merchandising rights can be extremely profitable. *Jurassic Park* merchandising is one such example. The typical studio net-profits definition, however, usually includes only a small amount of the revenues actually received by the studio from the exploitation of these rights. Studios do not like to give away any merchandising profits separate and apart from their net-profits definition. Still, there are exceptions, and sometimes the studio is forced to account separately to the original author for merchandising. This separate accounting is sometimes referred to as a "separate revenue stream." In such cases, either the work has been merchandised already, or it has the enormous and obvious potential to launch a very profitable merchandising business, such as *Star Wars* or *E.T.*

For instance, if you are selling motion picture and television rights to a comic book character which has already been established in the marketplace, you have a lot of leverage. The studio will still argue that the motion picture which they are going to produce will increase the merchandising potential and they want their piece. I do not know of any instances in which a studio is willing to walk away from some share of the merchandising business.

Negotiations are usually very difficult and take months. I have resolved several very difficult negotiations with the following formula: First, we established an existing level of merchandising revenues that existed before the studio bought any rights. That amount should *always* belong to the original creator. The studio certainly cannot argue that they are adding to an already existing market. The studio then will participate in all revenues *after* that level has been reached for a certain period of time, linked to the release of the picture—usually at least thirty-six months, starting six months prior to release of the picture. As an example, if *Batman* merchandising grossed $1,000,000 annually for the three years preceding release of the picture and grossed $3,000,000 annually after release of the picture, the studio would share in the additional $2,000,000 per year on merchandising, and on the characters already created prior to the production of the movie, during the time period that the studio is entitled to share in such revenues. Any merchandising based solely on the movie—such as any new characters created for the movie—will usually belong solely to the studio, and those revenues are included in the net profit pool, although sometimes one is able to get a separate piece of this merchandising as well. It is all negotiable.

The other big issue is who is actually going to do the merchandising. If the comic book character is already being merchandised, doesn't it make sense to have the same manufacturer continue to manufacture the merchandising for the movie? That is usually not a factor. The studio always wants control and will usually demand that the movie merchandising be arranged by the studio. They have their own relationships with merchandising companies and they prefer to work with their own people. At the very least, you should be able to continue merchandising those items already merchandised with the company that has been doing it. Any new merchandising items could be handled through the studio.

What if you have created material that you know has tremendous merchandising potential, but you have never done anything with it? In this case, it is doubtful the studio would let you reserve merchandising rights. You will be lucky if you can negotiate a separate merchandising royalty based solely on the merchandising revenues. In other words, if the picture is a flop, but the merchandising is profitable, the losses of the picture will not influence your right to receive money. However, in many instances, if you are successful in getting a separate merchandising royalty, the royalty may not be payable until the rest of the picture costs are recouped by the studio. In other words, your merchandising profits will accumulate based only on merchandising revenues and costs, but they do not actually get paid out unless the picture is successful.

The top royalty that the studio may pay is 15%–20% of *their* merchandising profits for characters that have already been merchandised. If the merchandising has never been exploited, the royalty will generally be much less. In defining merchandising profits, keep in mind that studios usually take a 50% fee for their services(!) in addition to a deduction for all of the merchandising costs. That fee may be justified or not. Some studios do license their own merchandising. Most use outside licensing agents. The licensing agents also take a fee on the revenue they receive— between 35%–50%. As an example, if $1.00 is received by the licensing agent and the licensing agent is receiving a 50% fee, they will take out $.50 for their fee and their costs of $.20. Thus, $.30 would be remitted to the studio. The studio takes off $.15 (50% fee) and costs of say $.05 from the $.30. That leaves $.10 and you get a piece of that. The trick is to put a cap on the combination of the licensing agent's and the studio's fee—maybe 65%. After all, only one of them is doing the real work. The other is just a middleman. This is a difficult area of negotiation, but if you have a lot of leverage, you may be successful. Note that the Writers Guild Agreement provides that a writer who has created a character that is merchandised must receive some separate compensation.

6. Holdbacks and the Right of First Negotiation/ First Refusal/Last Refusal

(a) *Holdbacks.* If you are successful in reserving certain rights, there are certain restrictions you must be willing to accept. If you have reserved production rights, such as stage rights, the studio will insist on a holdback of time before you are permitted to exploit your reserved rights. The rationale for the holdbacks is logical: if the studio is going to produce a picture based on your screenplay, they do not want a competing stage production to be playing at the same time. They want their picture to be the focus. This is a legitimate concern (unless they have purchased the rights to an existing play such as *A Chorus Line,* in which case they will not ask you to stop the run of the play). You, on the other hand, do not want to give the studio forever. This is also a legitimate concern. Both concerns are usually addressed. Studios customarily ask that you hold back *granting* stage rights for five years from release of the picture or seven years from exercise of the option, whichever is earlier. That way if the picture is never made, you will eventually be able to exploit these rights. You can sometimes knock this down to three (or four) years from the release of the picture (even two years if you have great leverage) or five (or six) years from exercise of the option, whichever is earlier. It is negotiable. The same holdbacks usually apply to live television and radio rights.

The restrictions concerning novelization rights are different. If there is no movie, there is no novelization. And if there is a movie, the studio does not want to hold back its publication. The studio does want to ensure, however, that you coordinate your novelization with the release of the picture. The publisher will have to agree to consult with the studio, use the studio graphics on the book, use certain language on the cover of the book (such as "See the upcoming Warner Bros. release") and release the book in conjunction with the release of the movie.

If you are successful in reserving merchandising rights, these will also have to be coordinated with the release of the picture, even if you are already merchandising a product.

(b) *First Negotiation/Last Refusal/First Refusal.* The studio will usually insist on the right to negotiate first to purchase your reserved rights when you offer them for sale. They have a vested interest and they want to know that they will have the first crack. This is called a "right of *first negotiation.*" But the right of first negotiation is usually not enough. You might ask $1,000,000 for the stage rights, a price they think is ridiculous. They do not want you to offer it to their competitor for $100,000, so they will ask for the right to match any other offer. This is called a "right of *last refusal.*"

Many writers feel that the right of last refusal effectively kills their ability to negotiate with anyone else. Other studios do not like to make an offer if someone can simply match it and pull the rug out from under them. While it is difficult to get around this, sometimes, again depending on how much leverage you have, you might be able to limit the studio's right to what some people call a "right of *first refusal.*" Keep in mind that there are many definitions of *first refusal* floating around and it should thus be carefully defined. Here is usually what is meant by it: You offer your stage rights to Warner Bros. for $1,000,000 and they counter with $500,000. You cannot then sell it to another studio for less than $500,000. If Columbia offers you $400,000, you have to go back to Warner Bros. and give them the right to match the offer. If someone offers you $550,000, on the other hand, then you can sell it. The argument is that Warner Bros. is sophisticated. They should have realized the value of the rights. They goofed in thinking that no one else would make a higher offer. Today, it is very difficult to get any studio to accept a first refusal right. However, sometimes they will accept a first refusal right with some room for error. No matter how sophisticated the studio is, it is hard to predict exactly what price a literary property will command in the marketplace. Thus, the studio will ask for the right to match any other offer, provided no one offers more than, say, 20% or 25% above their price. If an offer is made above that level, then the writer is free to take it. The studio was sufficiently off in its guess and loses its right. This provision is also difficult to get, but the argument does have some sound logic behind it and it is always worth a try.

There is one other variation to the last refusal and first refusal rights: The studio gets to match any other offer, but they have to pay 5% or 10% over that other offer. In other words, the studio has to pay a premium for their right.

7. Reserved Rights Generally

Today, with the cost of producing and releasing a picture so high, studios are reluctant to allow an author to reserve any meaningful rights. They want to be able to recoup their revenues from the so-called ancillary markets. If you are a writer for hire, the norm is that the studio will own everything. If you wrote the script on spec, as discussed above it may be possible to reserve stage, radio, and live TV rights. Novelization rights are harder if your work has never been published or you have never written a book before, but if you are a Guild member, you have certain protections in this area, and even if you are not, you can ask for them. Reserving the right to publish the screenplay is usually acceptable (but only if you are the sole writer), as there is not much money in it. The studio will usually allow you to reserve books on tape if you have written a book that they are purchasing.

With the cost of producing movies constantly going up, the studio's attitude toward reserved rights might change. And even though revenues are also going up, as of 1994 net revenues are starting to go down. Regardless, if the studio is buying a piece of your material that you have invested numerous hours in creating, then you should be entitled to reserve all heretofore customary reserved rights of authors. It's worth a fight.

E. REVERSIONS

How do you protect yourself if the studio buys your screenplay and sits on it—i.e., never makes a picture? Your goal is to have your screenplay turned into a movie—not to gather dust. What you want is a *reversion,* the ability to get your script back after a certain period of time if a picture is not produced. Studios *hate these*! Thus, it is very difficult, nearly impossible, to get this right. One basic reason is that the studio has already paid for your material. They feel they should get what they paid for, which means the rights. They also do not want to be embarrassed. The studio may have been indecisive. If you can take your material elsewhere and the next studio makes it a big hit, they look like fools. Studio executives do not like to look like fools, particularly when they are being paid huge bucks not to. Still, if you have leverage, you can ask for it. Reversions are much more common if you are selling a published book. At least you can argue that you had established a market for your material before the studio got involved and they cannot take forever to exploit it.

If the studio is open to the concept at all, they will probably want to hold on to your material for at least ten years, sometimes even a minimum of fifteen years, after the option is exercised, before your rights revert. It takes time to get a picture made and fewer are made each year. They have paid you what you wanted (remember, you did not have to sell your script to them) and they want time! They do not want a gun to their head.

If you are lucky enough to get a reversion, then the studio is bound to ask for their money back at some point in time. At the very least they will want back the money which they have actually paid to you plus interest. And not at the interest rate that you get paid in your savings account. The norm is 125% of the prime rate—in other words, a premium on top of the average interest rate charged over the period that the studio has expended money on the project. In the 1970s, with interest rates in excess of 15%, that sum could have been double or triple the amount paid.

What the studio will also ask for is to be paid back all of their costs—costs for messengers, writers, typists, et cetera. Try to eliminate these and to limit the payback to the money that has been paid to you only. If you have to pay for all these costs, then be sure that all rights in your material revert, including *all* of the subsequent screenplay drafts which the studio has commissioned. If you are paying for these rights, you should get them. (See also discussion below in subchapter O, regarding a reversion of your rewrites if the option on your initial screenplay lapses.)

"Wait"—you say—"the cost of this payback could be well in excess of my net worth!! Do I want this provision??" Do not worry. The studios are not interested in having *you* pay the bill. They want the next studio that you make a deal with to pay—when you set it up again. "But that may make it impossible for me to set up the project!!" you say. Again, do not worry—the next studio can negotiate with the first. Let them try to cut down the price if it is too much. The studios negotiate between themselves all the time and they will work it out if there is real interest. The studios have their own relationships with each other and what is good for the buyer is also good for the seller when the seller is on the buyer's side.

There are several types of reversions. Each is difficult to get. As noted above, the first reversion you should ask for is if the studio never makes a picture. What if they make a picture, but do not make a sequel? What if they make a sequel, but never make a television series? What if they make a TV series, but never make a movie? Look at *Batman, Dennis the Menace,* and *Star Trek.* Each project has been produced in several different media. Remember, also, that it took more than twenty years to make a movie out of the series in the case of *Batman* and *Dennis the Menace.* This is all negotiable, but if you believe your project has sequel or series potential, you might try to get some protection as follows: The studio, in essence, will get a rolling right to produce sequels and/or a television series. They have to commence production of a new film or television series within, say, ten years after release of the earlier production (in the case of a television series the time period would commence after production of the last episode) or they lose all subsequent production rights.

If you are a WGA member, you should be aware that the Guild in 1988 added a provision that allows the writer to get his rights back. Keep in mind that this right is very limited. It only applies to work which is original (not based on any preexisting material) and work which has not been exploited in any medium. The rule for literary material acquired after August 8, 1988 is that the writer may reacquire such material upon the expiration of five years following the later of (1) the studio's purchase or license of the material or (2) after the last draft is written *if* such literary material is not in active development. Note that once the studio is no longer in active development, it has a certain period of time to resume development again. If it does, then the cycle repeats itself. Once active development ceases, the writer can then proceed to reacquire the material (Writers Guild Basic Agreement, Section 16.A.8).

The best thing about the WGA provision is not just that it exists, which is a major accomplishment in itself, but that it exists for commissioned works as well as material that is purchased. If you are hired to write a script, you will *virtually never* see a reversion in a studio *contract*. The Guild provision is the only way to get your material back.

F. TRANSFER OF RIGHTS: EXERCISE OF OPTION

The most *important* aspect of any option/purchase or purchase contract (should you be lucky enough to sell a spec script outright) is the "transfer of rights provision." Note that when you option your screenplay, the effective purchase will take place if and when the option to purchase your screenplay is *exercised,* and at that time the rights which you are conveying to the other party will in fact be conveyed. What you want to ensure is that *payment accompanies* the transfer. In other words, the transfer of rights should be *subject* to your being paid the correct sum under the contract. If you do not get your money, the contract should not allow a transfer of rights. If the contract is worded poorly (I have seen contracts, for instance, which stipulate that the only requirement for exercise is notice to the author!) and a transfer of rights occurs without your being paid, then all you will end up with is a breach of contract suit for the purchase price if it is not paid. In other words, the buyer will own the rights and all you will have is the right to sue, which, believe me, will cost a lot of money for you to institute. You, of course, can argue that the failure to pay the purchase price negates the contract, but it is an argument, not a clean bill of health, so to speak, and under such circumstances, it would be difficult to enter into an agreement for that screenplay with another party.

Therefore, I always ensure that transfer will occur *when* payment is made. One major studio insists that they must have up to five days *after* the option is exercised to pay. I do not like this provision. On the other hand, since it is a major studio with major assets and since they will not change the provision, it is universally accepted. The major studios are trustworthy in this area. They would not be in business if they failed to pay for rights acquired. But you should *never,* ever, accept this provision if your contract is with an independent company. I've also seen transfer occurring on exercise of the option with payment on commencement of principal photography—in essence a perpetual right to pay. I've also seen contracts that include a provision that a transfer occurs on execution of the contract with a reversion if the studio doesn't pay a negotiated amount within a certain period of time. These provisions are to be avoided at all costs. Payment *must* accompany the exercise of an option or, if your contract is for the outright purchase of rights without an option, then with the transfer of rights. In short, purchase should only be effective if the requisite payment has been made.

Many option/purchase contracts are structured in two parts. There is a separate option contract and a separate purchase/transfer of rights contract which is attached to the option contract. You must sign *both*. While the purchase agreement states that you *are* transferring rights (the contract has language saying "I *hereby* grant Buyer the following rights"), there is also a provision in the option contract (at least there should be one) stating that the purchase contract is only effective *when the option is exercised.* (As noted above, this paragraph should also say when the option is exercised *and when the purchase price is paid.)* The provision usually goes on to say that the signature of the writer to the purchase contract will be void and have no effect unless the option is exercised and the purchase price is paid. If you negotiate nothing else in your agreement, this concept must be crystal clear. Otherwise you may end up in years of litigation and your project will be tied up.

Sometimes, the owner of a screenplay is able to negotiate further requirements for a transfer of rights to occur, such as that the purchaser must not only pay the purchase price, but also commence principal photography of a motion picture or hire a star or a director. These provisions are rare and you must have extraordinary bargaining power to get them. You should be aware, however, that such provisions exist.

G. SHORT-FORM DOCUMENTS: OPTION AND ASSIGNMENT

You will be asked to sign what is called a "short-form option agreement" and "short-form assignment," along with the option/purchase agreement. The purpose of the short-form option is for the purchaser to be able to file with the copyright office a short summary of the fact that your project is tied up and for how long. Once filed, it puts other buyers on notice of the agreement that has been entered into. The purpose of the short-form assignment is to record the fact that rights have been *granted*. The main reason that a short-form document is filed, instead of the longer contract, is (1) for simplicity and (2) so that the terms of the agreement are kept confidential. The studio does not want anyone to know what they have paid for their option and what the purchase price is, and for that reason neither do you. This is the same concept used with real estate sales. The purchase price of a house is never recorded.

The short-form option indicates the option periods. It usually looks something like this:

SHORT-FORM OPTION AGREEMENT

KNOW ALL MEN BY THESE PRESENTS: that in consideration of the payment of One Dollar ($1.00) and other good and valuable consideration, receipt whereof is hereby acknowledged, the undersigned, _____, does hereby sell, grant, assign and set over unto

_____ ("Purchaser"), and its heirs, representatives, successors and assigns forever, the exclusive and irrevocable right and option to purchase and acquire from the undersigned all rights throughout the world in perpetuity, in and to that certain original literary work described as follows:

Title:

Written by:

Publisher:

Date and Place of Publication:

Copyright and Registration No.:

including all contents thereof, all present and future adaptations and versions thereof, and the theme, title and characters thereof and in and to the copyright thereof and all renewals and extensions of such copyright.

The option herein granted may be exercised by Purchaser or his or its heirs, representatives, successors, licensees or assigns at any time on or before _____ or, if extended, as provided in that certain option agreement entered into concurrently herewith between Purchaser and the undersigned, at any time on or before _____, or if further extended on or before _____, and this agreement is subject to all of the terms, conditions and provisions contained in said agreement.

IN WITNESS WHEREOF, the undersigned has executed this assignment this _____ day of _____, 199_____.

_____
[Name]

The short-form assignment looks like this:

SHORT-FORM ASSIGNMENT

For good and valuable consideration, receipt whereof is hereby acknowledged, the undersigned hereby sells, grants and assigns to _____ ("Purchaser"), and its representatives, successors, and assigns, all right, title and interest, including the entire copyright and exclusive motion picture, television and allied rights throughout the world in perpetuity, in and to that certain original screenplay described as follows:

Title:

Written by:

including all contents thereof, all present and future adaptations and versions thereof, and the theme, title and characters thereof, as well as all subsequent production rights and in and to the copyright thereof and all renewals and extensions of such copyright.

The undersigned and Purchaser have entered into or are entering into a formal Agreement dated as of _____ relating to the transfer and assignment of the foregoing rights in and to said original screenplay, which rights are more fully described in said Agreement, and this Short-Form Assignment is expressly made subject to all of the terms, conditions and provisions contained in said Agreement.

IN WITNESS WHEREOF, the undersigned has executed this Short-Form Assignment this _____ day of _____, 199____.

_____
[Name]

Both documents should refer to the long-form agreement that you have entered into and be *subject* to all of the terms of that agreement. These documents are not meant

to modify in any way the terms that you have already negotiated. These documents are solely for recording purposes.
Indeed, it is crucial that these documents state that they
are subject to the terms of the longer agreement, and also,
in the event of any inconsistency between the short-form
and long-form documents, that the longer-form contract
prevails. As discussed in the previous chapter, for instance,
you want to make sure that no rights are assigned unless
the purchase price is paid. Having taken the time to see
that this provision is in your contract, you certainly do not
want the short-form assignment to upset the apple cart
and negate all of your negotiations.

Once these documents are recorded, anyone can
check with the copyright office concerning your project.
The easiest way is to call one of the handful of law offices
that specialize in copyright searches and to order a copyright report. Studios routinely order copyright reports
when they option and/or purchase literary properties.
They will give the name of the project and the name of the
writer. If the short-form option and assignments have been
filed properly, then these documents will be duly noted on
the report.

On a non-rush basis, such a report costs about $300.
If you want an opinion from a lawyer regarding the status
of the rights based on the copyright report, it will cost
approximately $350 more.

H. THE PURCHASE PRICE: FIXED COMPENSATION

How much you will be paid for your script is, of course,
negotiable. If you agree to option your script, you can try
for a higher purchase price than if it is to be purchased

outright. Argument: It's been taken off the market for the option period and will probably be shopped to everyone. Once shopped, a screenplay can lose its luster. (Many writers do not comprehend this and keep trying to sell the same old scripts. As a word of advice, once your script has been shopped, you must be selective about who you go to next with it. Find out who the script has been sent to. You do not want to pitch it to someone who has already passed. Then all that person will remember you for is that same old script which they did not like the first time and, believe me, that will not enhance your reputation.) The other argument to use in asking for a higher purchase price is that you have optioned your script for very little money. You gave them a break. Now they should give you one.

The amount you are to be paid for your script is the purchase price (also referred to as "fixed compensation," as distinguished from profits, which are referred to as "contingent compensation," because profits are contingent on the film's generating sufficient revenues).

The purchase price may also be split up into several components based on factors such as the budget of the movie, your final writing credit, and so on. The most important component, in my opinion, is the "exercise price." This is the price which must be paid by the end of the option period in order to purchase the rights. In my mind, this is the true purchase price. Once paid, you can never get your script back again unless you have a reversion (see discussion above). Many deals, however, do not include the entire purchase price in the exercise price and provide that the purchase price may be increased based on factors such as the budget of the picture and writing credit. These increases are really bonuses. But, in Hollywood jargon, these bonuses are actually spoken of as part of the purchase price. It makes it that much more difficult to figure out what is really being offered. Bonuses based on the budget of the picture and writing credit are nice, but they are paid when the picture is made, not at the time of exercise. The main thing to keep clear in your mind is *what* will you get paid if the picture is *never made,* and that is the exercise price. Ideally, you want as much of your ultimate compensation as possible included in the exercise price.

Sometimes a deal is structured so that a bonus is paid if the picture is made as a feature motion picture as distinguished from a television movie. The producer may not know when he options the script whether the picture will be a television movie or a feature. He might want to make it as a feature but keep his options open. If, after shopping the script, he cannot make a feature, then he wants the ability to make a television movie and that means a much lower price. In order to do this, the producer will set a low exercise price as the purchase price, which corresponds to the ultimate price to be paid if the picture is to be made as a television movie or a low budget movie. If the picture is eventually made as a feature or for a higher budget, then the producer will pay you more money at the time the picture is made. Of course, any such subsequent payments are all *speculative.* The picture may never be made.

Prices for two-hour network television spec scripts usually range from $40,000 to $75,000–$100,000 tops. Prices for other television productions are variable. For instance, a producer should pay more for a pay cable movie than for a network movie. Budgets for network movies are generally $2,500,000 on the average. Budgets for pay/cable movies are around $3,500,000 and go up to $5,000,000–$7,000,000 for special projects. Thus, if your purchase price for network TV is $50,000, try to get $65,000–$70,000 for pay TV. The producer might ask for a break for a non-pay, basic cable movie (e.g., USA Cable). Budgets for such movies are less—around $2,200,000. So, he might offer only $40,000–$45,000 for such a movie.

As an example, a producer might ask that the purchase price for network television be $50,000, pay cable $60,000, basic cable $40,000 and for features $150,000. For example, if, at the time of exercise, he knows he is probably going to make a network television movie, then he will pay you $50,000 at the time of exercise. If he ends up making the movie as a feature, he will pay you the balance when and if it gets made. (Remember, if you do not want to sell your script as a television movie, then do not even get into the distinction. That way, if the producer wants to make a television movie, he will have to pay you the feature price.)

1. Bonus Based on Budget

Assuming you will not be paid the maximum purchase price on exercise of the option, the easiest way to approach the issue of different media (feature versus television, pay TV versus network TV) and different budgets is to base the ultimate purchase price (including all bonuses) on the budget of the picture. You still need to establish a base exercise price to protect yourself if the movie is never made—a minimum price that must be paid by the end of the option period. The bonus based on a percentage of the budget will be paid when the budget is finalized.

Example: A producer has optioned your screenplay for three years. At the end of the three-year period, he must pay $100,000 to exercise the option or he loses his rights. If a picture based on your property is made and it is a $50 million movie, you will feel cheated if all you get is $100,000—so you build in some protection: 2 $1/2$% of the budget, with a floor of $100,000. The studio also insists on some protection, called a ceiling. The ceiling is usually no more than three times the exercise price. Of course, it is negotiable. Let's say the ceiling is $300,000. In this example, you would receive $300,000 for your script ($100,000 on exercise of the option, the balance when the final budget is established for the first picture based on your screenplay). You should always base the percentage on the "final" budget or, if possible, the final cost of the picture. Most studios will not base your bonus on the final cost, because if the picture goes over budget, they do not want to give you a premium based on their misfortune. They will usually agree to base your bonus on the final budget; however, excluding from the budget such items as interest and overhead.

2. Bonus Based on Credit

Another common provision is to give a bonus based on credit. There are usually two bonuses—one for sole screenplay credit, and one for shared screenplay credit. If you end up with either of these credits, a bonus should be paid. While this is an absolutely essential part of an employment agreement (when you are hired to write a script, as discussed in the next chapter), often the studio will argue that the bonus is already built into the purchase price, so you may not get this in an option/purchase situation. And, quite frankly, you want to get as much as you can up front (on exercise of the option). You are selling the rights —if they want to hire another writer, that is the studio's business. Your argument: You will not be happy unless you walk home with a guaranteed sum if the picture is made, no matter what credit you end up with. Bonuses, particularly a high sole screenplay bonus, only increase your chance of being kicked off the project at an early stage if the studio can find a cheaper writer.

If a screenplay bonus has to be part of the deal, meaning that some of your compensation will be paid based on credit, the number to focus on is the shared screenplay bonus. Nine times out of ten, you are going to be replaced and if you wrote the original script, odds are you will get shared screenplay credit (the Writers Guild determination procedure usually favors the original writer). The shared screenplay bonus is usually one half of the sole bonus. If you are worried about not getting any screenplay credit and therefore no bonus, then sometimes you can negotiate a bonus for just story credit. This sum will be lower, of course, than the screenplay bonuses. (See discussion in Chapter Three T on credit arbitration.)

In short, think about how much you are willing to accept if the picture is never made, how much you want guaranteed if the picture is made, and how much you are willing to risk based on credit, budget and the like. Be clear in your mind what your bottom line is in each instance.

I. CONTINGENT COMPENSATION: PROFITS

1. Percentages

Generally, writers who sell spec scripts are accorded 5% of 100% of the net profits. You always want to make sure it is "of 100% of *the* net profits." Otherwise, you will receive 5% of something that could be considerably less than 100% of all the net profits.

One pitfall you want to avoid is accepting a definition that says you will receive 5% of the "producer's net prof-its." Remember, the producer may retain only a small share (generally, producers receive 50% of 100% of the net profits, reducible by participations granted to actors, directors and the like—these persons are called "third-party profit participants"). The producer may or may not have a floor. As an example, if the producer's profits of 50% were reduced by third-party profit participants to 10%, you would receive 5% of 10%, or $1/2$% of 100% of *the* net profits—a far cry from the 5% of the profits that you thought you were getting. The producer may also be par-ticipating in the studio's gross and not receive net profits at all from the studio. Thus, a percentage of the pro-ducer's net profits may be non-existent.

You also want to make sure that the corporation you are contracting with is the corporation receiving the reve-nues from the picture. Let's say you are to receive 5% of 100% of the profits of Corporation A. Corporation A might be a so-called shell corporation—a corporation with no assets, designed principally to shield the individual pro-ducer from liability. The company with the assets may be a parent corporation of Corporation A, or the parent com-pany might be a separate company with no legal relation-ship to Corporation A whatsoever. When contracting with Corporation A, therefore, you should try to broaden the scope of the definition for purposes of defining your net profits. One solution is to say that you will receive 5% of 100% of the net profits of Corporation A, "its parents, subsidiaries, affiliates and related companies." This language takes into consideration the revenues which may be received by other companies not cited in your contract. Parent and subsidiary corporations have a definite legal and corporate relationship to the contracting entity. Affiliates and related companies may not, but the language is used as a catchall to prevent the producer or studio from squirreling away revenues without accounting to you for them. You will also want a guarantee from the parent corporation to protect any other compensation you are entitled to receive under the contract. If the shell corporation goes bankrupt, you'll probably be out of luck without the guarantee.

It happens often that you think you are going into business with a famous company. When you call the producer, the phones are answered indicating you have reached the famous company. You make a deal. Your contract arrives. The contracting entity is a company that you have never heard of. Obviously, there is some relationship. The famous company may even have issued a press release that they are doing your picture. The contract makes no mention of this famous company whatsoever. More likely than not, it is a related or affiliate company. The added language takes into account their revenues as well. You will probably want to spell out the famous company in your definition to avoid any doubt, but still use the affiliated or related company language to encompass companies that you may not be aware of. In this instance, you should receive "5% of 100% of the net profits of Corporation A, its parents and subsidiaries, famous company, its parents, subsidiaries and their respective affiliates and related companies."

Sometimes, the studios will not agree to give 5% of 100% of the profits to the seller of a spec script. But they will almost always agree to at least 2 $^1/_2$% of 100% of the net profits for the rights to the script and might stipulate that you will receive another 2 $^1/_2$% of 100% if you get sole screenplay credit. If you have leverage, you should be able to get 5% of 100% without regard to credit. You should also be able to get 5% of 100% of the net profits from the sale of a book. Since the book writer is usually not the writer of the screenplay, the book writer will not be able to get extra points for sole screenplay credit. So the norm has been 5%.

2. Definition

You have probably heard that "net profits" in Hollywood are almost non-existent. For the most part, this is true. But extremely successful pictures have generated net profits, so it is important for you to understand how they are defined. Many people incorrectly think that the studios keep different sets of books and do not report the actual earnings of a picture. If you understand what a net profits definition consists of, however, you will quickly realize that the studios do not have to hide anything. The definitions themselves make it almost impossible for a picture to reach the point where net profits are paid. This fact is largely what the famous Art Buchwald case was about.

One could probably write a whole book about net profits definitions. Many definitions are more than forty pages long, many in very small print. Since very few people in Hollywood have the leverage to negotiate them, and since those who do have leverage also have the clout to receive some type of gross definition, it is not necessary for you to understand every provision because you will not be able to change many of them anyway. What you should understand is why net profits are so *elusive*.

Net profits and gross participations are called "contingent compensation" (they are payable contingent on the picture making enough money to "breakeven" and may never be payable). They are also referred to as the "back end" or "points."

The studio does not pay profits until it reaches what is called "breakeven"—in simplistic terms, when it has made back its money. But making back its money does not mean that if it has spent $10,000,000 for a feature, the picture has grossed $10,000,000 at the box office. First of all, box office receipts are different from studio receipts. The studio (distributor) makes a deal with the movie houses (exhibitor) to play the picture. While there are many types of deals that exist between distributor and exhibitor, the general rule is that the distributor will end up with approximately 50% of the U.S. and Canadian box office receipts and somewhat less than that number from international distribution. Box office receipts are sometimes referred to as "gross at the source." The distributor's receipts are often called "film rentals" or "studio gross."

As you will see from the following example, if a picture costs $10,000,000 to make and earns $20,000,000 at the box office, it will still not reach breakeven. First, the distributor deducts its distribution fee. This is usually 30% for U.S. theatrical distribution. (The fees are higher for other media and foreign revenues.) Then it deducts the costs of distributing the picture (the costs of checking the receipts at the box office, the costs of collecting receipts, trade association dues, taxes other than corporate income taxes), conversion costs, residuals, licenses, duties and fees, and coop advertising charges (meaning ad costs that the studio and theater owners share). These costs are referred to as "off the tops." Then it deducts the costs of prints, advertising and marketing. A major film today is launched with an $8,000,000–$10,000,000 campaign. The studio imposes an overhead on advertising costs of usually 10%. Thus, if advertising costs are $5,000,000, add another $500,000. This fee is for the running of the studio ad department. (In the studios' minds, the distribution fee of 30% is not enough!)

Here is a sample provision of the type of expenses which the studio deducts:

(a) As used herein, the term Distribution Expenses shall mean all customary, direct, out-of-pocket and reasonable costs and expenses paid or incurred and thereafter paid by Studio or its subdistributors to the extent charged to Studio by its subdistributors, in connection with the distribution, advertising, exploitation and turning to account of the Picture of whatever kind or nature or other exercise of any of the rights granted to Studio under the Agreement, and shall include, without limitation, the following:

(i) All costs and expenses of release prints, replacements, duped and dubbed negatives, fine grains, interpositives, internegatives, sound, music or effects tracks, including rerecording of soundtracks, matrices, cassettes, tapes, duplicating material and other Picture material manufactured for use in connection with the Picture and television and theatrical trailers thereof net of any rebates, discounts and credits accorded to Studio, and all sums actually expended or incurred and thereafter paid by Studio in processing, inspecting, repairing and renovating said material, including, but not limited to, the repairing and renovating of reels, cans, containers and cassettes, all packing, shipping, storing, transportation and insurance costs, and all other expenses incurred in connection therewith; it being understood that Studio and its subdistributors may manufacture or cause to be manufactured as many or as few duped negatives, positive prints and other material for use in connection with the Picture as it or they, as the case may be, in their sole and absolute discretion, may consider advisable or desirable.

(ii) All costs and expenses of advertising, publicizing, promoting and exploiting the Picture and all rights therein, by such means to such extent as Studio may, in its sole discretion, consider advisable or desirable. Such advertising, publicity and exploitation expenses shall include, without limitation: payments for or in connection with the preparation, supervision and/or execution of advertising plans and campaigns; the preparation, supervision and production of theatrical and television trailers, teaser trailers, recordings and radio transcriptions; the preparation, supervision, printing and distribution of trade advertising and advertising for regional and national fan magazines and newspapers (including charges for space in such newspapers and magazines); the preparation, supervision and distribution of press books and all publicity, promotion and exploitation items, advertising accessories, lobby displays, slides, novelties and tie-ins; prerelease advertising and publicity, screenings and personal appearances by actors and/or other production personnel; so-called cooperative and/or theater advertising (other than for or by Studio directly); the salaries, costs and expenses of publicity and advertising personnel allocated on the basis of time spent on the Picture in relation to other films; artwork, posters and other accessories, still photographs and other advertising material used in connection with the Picture; the salaries of field exploitation personnel allocated on the basis of time spent on the Picture and their expenses; any film festival or market expenses or other selling or nonselling activities related to the Picture; and any such expenses incurred in connection with "four-wall" exhibition and any excesses of "four-wall" expenses over "four-wall" film rentals received. All marketing costs to be advanced by Studio are to be recouped as a distribution expense from the balance of monies due after deducting commission. Except as set forth in this paragraph, no salary or fee paid to any permanent executive of Studio shall be deductible as a Distribution Expense.

(iii)   All costs and expenses of preparing and delivering the Picture for distribution in any and all media, now known or hereafter devised (including, without limitation, salaries and expenses of parties not regularly employed by Studio), including, without limitation, all costs incurred in connection with the production of foreign language versions of the Picture, whether dubbed, subtitled, superimposed or otherwise, as well as any and all costs and expenses in connection with the changing of the title of the Picture, the recutting, reediting, dubbing, redubbing, shortening or lengthening of the Picture for release in any territory or for television sales and exhibition on television or in any other media, or for videogram sales or renting, or in order to conform to the requirements of censorship authorities or to the peculiar national or political prejudices likely to be encountered in any territory, or for any other purpose or reason, subject to the Agreement. The costs and expenses referred to in this subparagraph (iii) shall (A) include all studio charges for facilities, labor and material, whether or not incurred at a studio owned or controlled by Studio, and all costs and expenses of delivery materials; (B) be net of laboratory negative and print discounts for only the Picture and advertising agency commission rebates relating to only the Picture and (C) not include any markup for Studio's own benefit. Except as set forth in this paragraph, no salary or fee paid to any permanent executive of Studio shall be deductible as a Distribution Expense.

(iv) All sums paid, incurred or accrued on account of sales, use, receipts, income, excise, remittance and/or any other taxes or license fees, however denominated, imposed, assessed or levied by any governmental authority or duly constituted taxing authority, imposed, assessed or levied upon the negatives, duplicate negatives, prints or sound recordings of the Picture, or upon the use or distribution of the Picture, or upon the revenues derived therefrom or any part thereof, or upon the remittance of such revenues or any part thereof (but not including any taxes based solely on Studio's net income or accrued on account of duties, customs and imposts, costs of acquiring permits and any similar authority to secure the entry, licensing, exhibition, performance, use or televising the Picture in any country or part thereof, regardless of whether such payments, charges or accruals are assessed against the Picture or the proceeds thereof or against a group of motion pictures in which the Picture may be included or the proceeds thereof). In no event shall the recoupable amount of any such tax (however denominated) imposed be decreased (nor the Gross Receipts increased) because of the manner in which such taxes are elected to be treated by Studio in filing net income, corporate franchise, excess profits or similar tax returns. Subject to the foregoing, Participant shall not be required to pay or participate in (A) Studio's own income taxes and franchise taxes based on Studio's net income; or (B) any income tax payable to any country or territory by Studio based on the net earnings of Studio in such territory or country and which is computed and assessed solely by reason of the retention in such country or territory by Studio of any portion of the Gross Receipts. Gross Receipts shall include an amount equal to any refund received by Studio of taxes paid by Studio and deducted as a Distribution Expense pursuant to this paragraph

(iv) and, to the extent Studio shall have not deducted a distribution fee on Gross Receipts inclusive of such taxes, Studio shall not deduct a distribution fee on such refund.

(v) All costs and expenses of converting and transmitting to Los Angeles, California, any funds accruing to Studio in respect of the Picture from foreign countries, including, without limitation, cable expenses and any discounts from such funds taken to convert such funds directly or indirectly into United States Dollars or Pounds Sterling;

(vi) All costs and expenses of contesting any of the matters described in subparagraphs (iv) and (v) above, with a view to reducing the same, which costs shall be fairly apportioned to the Picture (on a mathematically justifiable basis) if done on an industry-wide basis or with respect to motion pictures distributed by Studio generally);

(vii) If the Picture is distributed theatrically, all costs and expenses paid or incurred in collecting Gross Receipts, including, without limitation, attorneys' fees and all costs and expenses of checking attendance and receipts at any and all theaters where Studio may be exhibited and all costs and expenses of checking and analyzing percentage engagements, accountings and payments of film rental in connection with the Picture under percentage engagements with exhibitors of the Picture; provided, however, that if the expenses of such box office analysis of motion pictures other than the Picture are included with such expenses in connection with the Picture, then the amounts set forth in this reasonable and customary basis, and to the extent Studio (rather than a subdistributor or licensee of Studio) shall make such allocation, such allocation shall be made in good faith and on a mathematically justifiable basis;

(viii) All amounts paid or incurred to or for the benefit of actors, writers, directors and others pursuant to applicable collective bargaining agreements by reason of any exhibition or exploitation of the Picture in any media in the Territory, or by reason of, or as a condition for, any use, reuse or rerun thereof for any purpose or in any manner whatsoever including, without limitation, royalties, participations and re-use fees (hereinafter collectively referred to as "residuals"), and all taxes, pension, health and welfare fund contributions, and other costs and payments computed on or payable in respect of any such residuals. To the extent reasonably practicable, all residuals paid by Studio that are in respect of a particular exploitation of the Picture shall be included on the accounting statement(s) in which Studio accounts for the Gross Receipts derived from such exploitation, it being agreed that Studio has no obligation to pay any residuals;

(ix)   All costs and expenses of errors and omission insurance incurred by or on behalf of Studio and thereafter paid (including, without limitation, any extensions Studio obtains of Producer's errors and omissions insurance or additional or supplementary coverage), it being understood, however, that Studio shall not be obligated to secure or maintain any such insurance;

(x)   All costs and expenses of securing and maintaining copyright protection for the Picture throughout the Territory, including, without limitation, the cost of copyright and title reports and copyright registrations and renewals and extensions thereof;

(xi)   Dues, fees, assessments and contributions (to the extent paid, incurred or accrued and allocated to the Picture or the distribution thereof) to the Motion Picture Association of America or other motion picture and/or television industry trade organization of which Studio or any subdistributor may now be or hereafter become a member.

(xii) All costs and expenses paid or incurred (and thereafter paid) in connection with any claims, actions, suits, pro-
ceedings, litigation, arbitration or other disputes (hereinafter
collectively referred to as "Claims") arising out of or in connection with the Picture, including, without limitation, Claims
relating to infringement, unfair competition, violation of
prints or other material, violation of any Guild provision, material on which the Picture is based or otherwise in exhibition
of the Picture. Without limiting the generality of the foregoing, the expenses described in this subparagraph (xii) shall
include all outside attorneys' and accountants' fees, investi-
gative costs and fees, losses, costs, damages (including the
gross amount[s] paid for the settlement of any Claims or on
account of any judgment, decree or decision relating to any
Claims) or other liabilities paid or incurred (and thereafter
paid) in connection with any such Claims;

(xiii) If any person or entity shall make a Claim relating
to the Picture against Studio and/or any of its licensees,
which Claims, in Studio's judgment, is of sufficient merit or
constitute a reasonable probability of ultimate loss, cost,
damage or expense, Studio may deduct as a Distribution Expense the amount of any liability, loss, cost, damage or expense suffered as a result thereof. Subject to the Agreement,
Studio shall have the right to settle and pay any such Claim.
After the settlement of any such Claim, or after the final judi-
cial determination thereof, the amount previously deducted
hereunder shall be adjusted accordingly with the next accounting statement rendered hereunder. Nothing herein
contained shall be construed as a waiver of any of Participant's representations or warranties contained in the Agreement to which this Exhibit is attached, or as a waiver of any
right or remedy at law or otherwise which may exist in favor
of Studio, including, but not limited to, the right to require
Participant to reimburse Studio on demand for any loss, liability, cost, damage or expense arising out of, or resulting

from, any breach by Participant of its representations, warranties, covenants and/or other agreements, or any right on the part of Studio to set off, recoup or recover any such cost or expense out of or against Participant's share of any monies payable hereunder other than the Purchase Price, rather than treating such costs or expenses as Distribution Expenses hereunder.

(xiv) All other costs and expenses actually paid or incurred (and thereafter paid) by Studio in connection with the distribution, promotion, advertising, publicizing and/or exploitation of the Picture or any rights granted to Studio in the Agreement.

(b) Whenever Studio makes an expenditure or incurs (and thereafter pays) any liability in respect of films, including the Picture, or any right therein, pursuant to any agreement or arrangement which does not specify what portion of the expenditure or liability applies to the respective films in the group, then in any and all such situations, Studio shall deduct as a Distribution Expense such sums as Studio shall determine reasonably in good faith.

(c) To the extent the Picture is distributed by a subdistributor, the term *Distribution Expenses* shall include (in addition to any of the foregoing costs and expenses which may be incurred by Studio) all costs and expenses incurred by Studio in connection with entering into and administering the contract with each such subdistributor. To the extent the Picture is distributed by a subdistributor, all Distribution Expenses of the type or nature described in this Paragraph 5 incurred by such subdistributor and passed on to Studio or which Studio otherwise accepts for purposes of its accountings with such subdistributor shall be deducted by Studio from Gross Receipts for purposes of determining Producer's Profits hereunder, as if Studio had incurred such expenses without any cap. Notwithstanding the foregoing, the term

Distribution Expenses, as used herein, shall not include any cost or expense paid or incurred by a subdistributor of the Picture if:

(i)   such cost or expense was applied against and deducted from gross receipts derived in respect of the Picture by such subdistributor; and

(ii)   the gross receipts against which such costs and expenses were applied were excluded from the computation of Gross Receipts.

Let's say that these distribution expenses total $13,000,000.

Using our example, here is where we're at:

If the picture has grossed $20,000,000 at the box office, and distribution costs = $13,000,000 ($5,000,000 of that for advertising), then:

```
Film Rentals = $20,000,000
  × 50%                        = − $10,000,000
Distribution Fee (30%)         = −     3,000,000
                                      7,000,000
Distribution Costs             −    13,000,000
Ad Overhead (10% ×
$5,000,000)                    −       500,000
                               − $  6,500,000
```

Suppose the film grosses $10,000,000 at video stores. You probably think the film has reached breakeven. WRONG! The studios have an obnoxious policy regarding video revenues. Only a small portion of the revenues go into the pot for purposes of calculating profits. The norm is that the studios will include a 20% royalty into gross. (Some studios take a distribution fee off of that, but for purposes of this computation, let's assume they don't.) The twenty percent royalty is based on the *wholesale* selling price, not retail. Let's say of the $10,000,000 grossed at retail video stores (through sales and rentals), $6,500,000 represents the wholesale selling price of those cassettes. Twenty percent of $6,500,000 = $1,300,000. Now the studios sometimes take a distribution fee off of that.

Let's use our example of 30%.

	$1,300,000
Less Distribution Fee	− 390,000
(30% × $1,300,000)	
	$ 910,000

Out of $10,000,000 in sales, only $910,000 is calculated into gross. Using our example:

Film Rentals	$10,000,000	
Less Distribution Fee	− 3,000,000	
		$7,000,000
Add Video Royalty	+ 1,300,000	
		$8,300,000
Less Video Distribution Fee	− 390,000	
		$7,910,000
Less Distribution Costs	−13,000,000	
Less Ad Overhead	− 500,000	
Studio Gross		−$5,590,000

You now see why the concept of net profits is elusive.

The other major killer deduction is the interest that is charged until the picture breaks even. Interest is charged on the unrecouped cost of the picture. (The entire interest charge is recouped first before the other deductions, unlike a mortgage on a house.) Sometimes the studio also charges an overhead fee on top of the cost of the picture. Let us say film rentals and video monies and other revenues derived from the picture, less distribution costs and distribution fees, equals $10,000,000. In our example, that is also the cost of the picture. Has the studio broken even? No way. By that point, our $10,000,000 picture cost (the industry term for picture cost is *negative cost)* is not $10,000,000. Say the studio charges a 12 1/2% overhead fee (they sometimes charge as much as 17 1/2%). The $10,000,000 negative cost is now $11,250,000 without adding the interest charge. Interest charges can be quite high. Keep in mind that the studio does not charge the actual rate of interest which it is charged by its bank. It usually charges 125% of the prime rate charged by the bank. In other words, it makes a profit on the interest! If the prime rate is 8%, the interest rate charged is 10% on the *unrecouped* portion of the negative cost, until all receipts less distribution costs are enough to pay back the negative cost. Interest charges are recalculated as additional revenues are received, but until recoupment, you know that interest is always charged on the unrecouped portion of the negative cost. As you can see, the interest cost could add up to $1,000,000 *per year,* thus pushing the point of recoupment farther and farther back. Most studios charge interest on overhead, some overhead on interest.

There is one other key deduction which also makes it

almost impossible ever to see net profits. In order to understand this deduction, first you must understand the basic difference between a "net profit participant" (one who is entitled to a share of net profits) and a "gross participant" (one who is entitled to a share of gross as opposed to net). There are several types of gross participants. The best gross participant definition is for the participant who receives gross from the first dollar. This person receives a share of the studio's gross, less *only* the off-the-top deductions (listed above), which such "off-the-tops" usually amount to approximately 5%. Thus, if the studio gross is $10,000,000 and the off-the-tops are $500,000 (5% × $10,000,000), the dollar-one gross participant will receive a percentage of the initial $9,500,000 that the studio receives. The net participant, on the other hand, receives a share of $9,500,000 less a 30% distribution fee, less all the other deductible costs. Using our example, a share of nothing.

There are few dollar-one gross players. Most persons who receive gross receive what is called an "adjusted gross." Adjusted gross is basically the same as net profits with one major exception: The distribution fees are lowered, in some cases to 15%. As noted above, the distribution fee for theatrical rentals is usually 30% (for U.S. rentals); the Distribution Fee for foreign theatrical receipts is usually 40%. Television can be higher. The distribution fee on U.S. cable receipts is usually 35%. The general rule is that the *average* full distribution fees on all receipts (domestic and foreign, theatrical and television) is 34%. Thus, reducing the fees to 15% on all receipts can make a huge difference.

As an example, for net profit participants, if studio gross is $10,000,000, then you normally deduct 34% for distribution fees (the average of all distribution fees), or $3,400,000, leaving $6,600,000 to be applied toward recoupment of expenses and negative cost. If only 15% of $10,000,000, or $1,500,000, is deducted, that leaves $8,500,000 toward recoupment of expenses and the negative cost, which means that the picture will reach breakeven much earlier.

Now that you understand the basic difference between net and gross participants, you should be aware that *gross* participations are also deducted in calculating *net* profit participation breakeven. Using our example above:

Rentals	$10,000,000	
Less Distribution Fee	− 3,000,000	
		$7,000,000
Add Video Royalty	+ 1,300,000	
		$8,300,000
Less Distribution Fee (Video)	− 390,000	
Studio Gross		$7,910,000
Less Distribution Costs	−13,000,000	
Less Ad Overhead	− 500,000	
		−$5,590,000

Now let us say gross participations of $1,000,000 were paid out before net profit breakeven is reached. The studio sometimes charges interest and overhead on these participations, too, so the $1,000,000 could turn into $1,300,000 or more. You deduct these gross participations from the bottom line also (because the studio treats them as if they were part of the negative cost), so the −$5,590,000 becomes −$6,890,000.

There are other provisions that are just as egregious, if not more so. (For instance, the distribution fee for merchandising is 50% and the studios sometimes hire an outside merchandising agent to take care of the licensing. That outside agent also takes a fee. If his fee is 30%, you have in essence close to an 80% fee on merchandising receipts!) I could go on for pages—that is the subject of another book. Hopefully, you get the idea why artists are outraged about not getting profits.

J. WHAT YOU CAN NEGOTIATE

There are very few provisions that one can negotiate in a net profits definition, particularly if you are just beginning your career. However, there are two important provisions you should negotiate, and can get, if you ask for them. Most net profits definitions provide for a penalty if the picture goes over budget. This provision is basically designed as an incentive for the director and producer to bring the picture in on budget. The provision is called a "double addback" because the studio adds twice the over-budget amount to the negative cost in its calculations. Writers have absolutely nothing to do with whether a picture comes in on budget or not, so this provision can be deleted.

The other provision concerns cross-collateralization and abandonment charges. Some producers and directors have what they call "overall deals" at a particular studio. The reason they are called overall deals is that the deals contemplate that the individual will make or be involved in more than one picture at that studio. The producer may be exclusive to that studio or he/she may have an obligation to bring the projects to that particular studio first. Some studios link the pictures (total or partial) for purposes of recoupment, although this is uncommon. If picture #1 is produced and unrecouped, the studio may require that the second picture earn enough revenues so that they get back their money on the first picture out of revenues from picture #2 before they pay profits on the second picture. Or they may simply want to recoup from picture #2 the monies that they *paid* the producer or director with an overall deal on picture #1. The studio may also allocate a portion of the overhead expenses of a producer with an overall deal to each picture that he produces. These charges also may be charged to the writer: secretaries, office messengers and the like. The recoupment of one picture's losses from another picture's profits in the calculation of a film's profits or a producer's fees and expenses is called cross-collateralization. As the writer usually does not have an overall deal, the cross-collateralization charges which may be deducted for a director or producer should not be charged to the writer.

Finally, the producer with an overall deal may have developed a project that was abandoned. The studio may charge off all of the costs of this abandoned project to a picture that is produced, for purposes of deferring the producer's profits on the picture so produced. These charges are called "abandonment charges" and the writer should not be charged in the calculation of the writer's profits on that picture.

Another point you can usually negotiate in a net profits definition is the time period you have to sue with respect to profit participation statements (i.e., if you think the revenues reported are inaccurate or the calculations are wrong). The studio definition usually gives you twelve months. This can be increased to up to twenty-four to thirty-six months. Accounting periods are usually the same for everyone (quarterly for at least the first year, semiannually thereafter for several years, then yearly).

Producers, directors, and some high level writers can also negotiate other provisions in a net profits definition, which may or may not make a difference. Some studios accept a cap or a ceiling on collection and checking costs (1% of gross revenues for each). Some studios accept a cap on Motion Picture Association and other trade association dues; the studio pays dues for all of its pictures, so it is unfair for them to charge off all of these costs for your picture. (Caps are sometimes $50,000–$75,000 for U.S. trade dues and the same for foreign trade dues.) Some studios, although it is rare, put a cap on the overhead. Some studios agree not to charge overhead on interest charges and interest on overhead charges. Some studios eliminate the distribution fee on the video royalty. Some non-major studios may increase the customary 20% video royalty. Some studios agree not to charge off the salaries of their in-house employees (arguably that is what the distribution fees and overhead charges should cover). Or, sometimes, the studio will agree not to charge interest or overhead on gross participations. Some studios agree that their fees are inclusive of subdistributor and subagent fees. This is an important provision because subdistributors may charge the same or a greater fee than the studio, in which case you have fees on top of fees, which gets ridiculous! Recall the discussion at the beginning of this subchapter regarding parent, subsidiary, affiliates and related companies. At the very least, you want to ensure that each affiliate company is not taking a separate distribution fee. Just as the catchall is used to provide that your net profit definition takes into consideration the revenues derived from all such companies, the definition should also make certain that the distributor fees set forth in the net profit definition include the fees of all such companies.

The other big issue concerns the inclusion of advances into gross (what we often call "the pot") for purposes of determining the net. Many companies will receive an advance for the sale of pay cable rights or home video rights. They may receive this when the picture is completed. Most definitions do not include these advances in the calculation of gross when they are received. Rather, they include the revenues from these sources when and if they are *earned*. For example, pay cable receipts will be included when the movie is broadcast on pay cable. Similarly, the company may have received an advance against home video sales. This will not be included for two reasons. First, the calculation of home video revenues for you is different than for the studio (see discussion above). For the most part, the studio receives 100% of the wholesale video revenues from the retailer—not the 20% royalty you will receive). Second, your calculation will be based on videocassettes actually sold. The company may receive an advance which represents sales of 100,000 cassettes. It is a non-returnable advance, but you do not get the benefit of it. If only 20,000 units are sold, your definition only takes into account sales of 20,000 cassettes and not the 100,000 which the company received monies for. These provisions will not be changed. However, sometimes the studio will agree, as a compromise, that for purposes of calculating interest charges only, the money that the studio receives as an advance will be deemed received, and therefore you will not be charged interest on the money. In other words, for purposes of calculating your share, the studio did not receive the money, but for purposes of calculating interest charges, they did. Now you see why studios do not have to keep various sets of books. The unfavorable bookkeeping is built into the definition.

The producer is usually in a better position to negotiate, so many writers ask to be tied to the producer's definition. If you make a deal with a producer before he takes a project to the studio, you have no way of knowing which studio definition, if any, you will be stuck with. If the producer agrees to tie you to his net definition (which most will), make sure the contract specifies that you will not be charged any over-budget penalties or cross-collateralization charges. Remember, too, that you will only be tied to the producer's *net* definition. If he gets gross, his gross definition will not apply to you. Try to find out if the producer you are going into business with is a "gross player" —one who receives "gross" as distinguished from "net." Your agent or lawyer will probably know. Note that if you are tied to the producer's definition, you might not get your own audit rights. The producer may agree to give you the same definition of profits he has, but say to you he will not let you audit the studio separately. In that case, you want to be able to "piggyback" on his audit rights—in short, to join him when he audits the studio and pay the proportionate costs. You also want to be able to cause him to audit the studio, even if he does not want to. But in this case, you will have to bear all the costs unless the producer decides to join in.

K. DEFERMENTS

Deferments are delayed payments. They can either be fixed—in which case they are payable on a certain date—or contingent—in which case they are payable contingent on certain circumstances, such as the film earning enough money to reach net profits.

An example of a fixed deferment would be a payment of a certain amount that is required to be made within one year after the option is exercised, regardless of whether a film is produced. If the option is exercised, it *must* be paid. Such deferments are rare in writers' deals. The only reason for you to take a fixed deferment, in lieu of cash on exercise of the option, is to give the purchaser a breather in respect of his payment obligations.

An example of a contingent deferment would be a payment of an agreed-upon sum out of the first net profits of the picture. The deferment would be paid before any net profit participations are paid out of the first monies that are available to net profit participants. Suppose you are a net profit participant entitled to a 5% share: then if, for example, $100,000 in net profits are generated, you would be entitled to $5,000. But if there are any deferments, these have to be paid first. If you have a $100,000 deferment payable out of the first net profits and $100,000 in net profits are generated, then, assuming you are the only person entitled to a deferment, you would receive the $100,000 (this also assumes that there are no other charges tacked onto the deferment—in many cases the studio treats the deferment as if it were part of the negative cost and adds overhead and interest charges!). No net profits would be payable because the net profits generated are eaten up by the deferment in this example. If others are entitled to deferments, then usually all deferments are paid out on a pro rata basis. Thus, if another person is also entitled to a $100,000 deferment and $100,000 of net profits is generated, you would each receive $50,000 out of the first $100,000. You would also each receive another $50,000 out of the next $100,000 of net profits.

L. PASSIVE PAYMENTS

When you sell a script to a studio or write a screenplay for a studio, they will purchase *all* rights, other than the limited reserved rights generally allowed and, specifically, the ones that you have negotiated. What if the studio produces a sequel picture or a television series based on the script? Shouldn't you be entitled to something? The answer is yes and studios will give you something if you ask. A production following the initial production is commonly called a "subsequent production." The payments for these subsequent productions are called "passive payments," because you do not have to *do* anything to receive payments. Payment is automatic, but there are usually conditions.

If you sell a screenplay, passive payments should be unconditional, but often they are not. Certainly if you are commissioned to write a screenplay, and often if you sell a screenplay, the studio will require that the first picture produced be comprised essentially of your story and characters. Under the WGA rules you must be accorded what are called "sole separated rights." If the script has been dramatically changed in its plot and characters, you may only receive "shared separated rights," which in most cases will *not* entitle you to a passive payment or, at best, will entitle you to a reduced royalty. Some studios require also that you receive sole "written by" or sole "screenplay by" credit. There are numerous combinations. The general rule is that in order to receive passive payments, you must at least receive sole separated rights. (If the studio does give passive payments for shared separation of rights, the payments are usually one half of the payment accorded for sole separated rights. If the studio does accord payments for shared separated rights, you can also ask to have the sole-separated-rights passive payment reduced by the amounts paid to other writers entitled to shared separated rights to a floor of one half the passive payment for sole separated rights. That way, if the other writers' payments are considerably less than yours, you might not be reduced to your floor.) Studios that award passive payments for sole "written by" or "screenplay by" credit will usually reduce the payment by one half for shared "screenplay by" credit. Ideally, you want to provide for payment one way or another if you receive sole or shared separated rights or sole or shared screenplay credit, so try to get it.

If you sell a script, try to get passive payments without hitches. After all, you do have some leverage if you are selling your script. Remember, you do not have to sell it and it is fair to say that if your script is turned into a feature and a sequel and maybe another sequel and/or a television series, you get something, regardless of credit and regardless if the script is changed. If you are being hired to write, you have less leverage, so undoubtedly you will have to live with whatever conditions the studio imposes. All studios have different policies and these policies are sometimes changed (usually not in your favor, but sometimes so).

Most importantly, you want passive payments for sequels and remakes. The general rule is that you get 50% of what you were paid for the first picture for each sequel produced and 33 $\frac{1}{3}$% for a remake. Make sure that it is 50% and 33 $\frac{1}{3}$%, respectively, of the *entire* compensation you were paid for the first picture, including the *bonuses*. Usually, the initial contract presented by the studio does not refer to the bonus. The moral here is *ask and you shall receive*. The accepted standard is that your passive payment is based on *all* of your compensation, including the screenplay bonus, budget bonus and the like. As an example, if you received $180,000 including bonuses on the first picture, you will receive $90,000 for a sequel and $60,000 for a remake. Again, you should not have to do anything. Payment should be automatic.

You should also receive 50% and 33 $\frac{1}{3}$% (for sequels and remakes, as applicable) of the contingent participation you were entitled to receive on the first picture. Thus, if you were entitled to 5% of the net profits on the first picture, you will be entitled to 2 $\frac{1}{2}$% of the net profits for a sequel.

You should also negotiate passive payments for a television series. In television, these are commonly called "episodic royalties" (they are paid for each original episode produced). There are usually three different figures: one for a thirty-minute series, one for an hour series and one for a ninety-minute series. There are no ninety-minute series today and this is a holdover from days gone by, but it is still negotiated. Low end writers will receive in the realm of $1,250–$1,750 per episode for a thirty-minute series, $1,500–$2,000 per episode for a sixty-minute series and $1,750–$2,250 per episode for a ninety-minute series. At the high end, the figures start at $2,000–$2,500 and increase to $3,500–$5,000 or more (although anything over

$3,000 is high even for top writers). The range is not that big.

The series royalty payment is generally for a network (ABC, NBC, CBS) show, broadcast in prime time in the U.S. Try to get Fox, and the new Warner Bros. and United Paramount included as networks, although some studios will not accept it. Try also to get 50% of the respective payments for non-network or non–prime time shows. Most studios will accept this. In other words, if the royalty is $1,500 per episode for a network prime time show, the royalty would be $750 per episode for a non-network or non–prime time show.

Additionally, you should also be entitled to a royalty for reruns of a series. The norm is to receive the same episodic royalty that you received for the first series episode again as payment for the first five reruns. This is called "100 over 5." It is payable in installments, in other words, 20% of the royalty for each rerun.

Royalties are also paid for spin-offs. There are two types of spin-offs: "generic" and "planted." A "generic spin-off" is a television production that is primarily based upon another television production that is itself a remake of or sequel to the first series and which features, as the primary characters in such spin-off, characters that appeared as primary characters in the first production. A "planted spin-off" is one based on a previous series and which presents as its essential continuing character one which was neither contained in the first series nor as a continuing character in the previous series. Royalties for generic spin-offs are usually 50% of the applicable royalties that you negotiate for the first television series, and for a planted spin-off, 25% of the applicable royalties. Thus, if your royalty for a 30-minute network prime time broadcast is $1,500 for the first television series produced based on your work, then the royalty for a 30-minute network prime-time generic spin-off episode is $750, and $375 for a similar planted spin-off.

You can also negotiate a passive payment for a television movie of the week or miniseries that is produced after the first film. Figures start at $5,000 an hour and go up to $15,000 or more per hour for top writers. There is usually a cap of six hours. (In other words, if the miniseries is eight hours, you only get paid for six hours. Using $5,000 per hour as an example, you will be paid $30,000.) Some studios accept a cap of eight hours and it is rare that a miniseries will be longer than that. You can also try for the "100 over 5" rerun formula with respect to reruns of the movie-of-the-week or miniseries. Generally, the studio will not accept an additional rerun payment for these productions. Your payment, in other words, is a buyout of all reruns. If you are a member of the WGA, the WGA does provide for payment for reruns, however.

Usually, even though you are entitled to profits from the first picture, you will not be entitled to receive profits from a series or a subsequent movie-of-the-week or miniseries, but it does not hurt to ask. If the buyer is an independent producer and you have leverage, you may succeed. And if you have a lot of leverage at a studio, you may succeed.

Here is a sample of a passive payment section from a contract:

ADDITIONAL CONSIDERATION: In addition to the basic consideration provided for above, (a) If Owner is not in material default of this Agreement, and (b) Owner is entitled to sole separation of rights under the WGA Agreement with respect to the Picture, and (c) Owner is not engaged to render writing services in connection with the applicable production, then Purchaser agrees to make contingent and supplemental payments to Owner based upon certain events and certain uses of the Work as follows:

(a) In the event Purchaser shall produce a feature-length motion picture intended for initial theatrical release based upon the Work pursuant to the rights granted (or agreed to be granted) to Purchaser pursuant to this Agreement, and shall thereafter produce a "remake" of such motion picture (i.e., a feature-length motion picture intended for initial theatrical release, which contains substantially the same story and the same leading characters as contained in the Work and used in said motion picture), Purchaser shall pay to Owner the additional sum of one third ($\frac{1}{3}$) of the Purchase Price not later than commencement of principal photography of such remake.

(b) In the event Purchaser shall produce a feature-length motion picture intended for initial theatrical release based upon the Work pursuant to the Agreement, and shall thereafter produce a "sequel" of such motion picture (i.e., a feature-length motion picture intended for initial theatrical release, which contains substantially the same leading characters, but a substantially different story than contained in the Work), Purchaser shall pay to Owner the additional sum of one half ($\frac{1}{2}$) of the Purchase Price not later than commencement of principal photography of such sequel.

(c) In the event Purchaser shall produce a feature-length motion picture intended for initial theatrical release based upon the Work pursuant to the rights granted (or agreed to be granted) to Purchaser pursuant to this Agreement or a television motion picture, and shall thereafter produce a feature-length motion picture based upon the Work intended for initial exhibition on U.S. free network television, Purchaser shall pay Owner the sum of $7,500 pursuant to the rights granted (or agreed to be granted) to Purchaser pursuant to this Agreement in respect of each such motion picture having a running time of one hour or less, and $7,500 per hour for each hour in excess of the first hour; provided, however, that in no event shall the maximum aggregate amount payable under this paragraph (c) exceed $50,000. Purchaser and Owner acknowledge that the amount payable hereunder is separate from any compensation payable pursuant to paragraph (b) above.

(d) In the event a television series (excluding a "miniseries," "movie-of-the-week" or the Picture itself) is produced by Producer based on the Picture for initial prime time network (U.S.) exhibition, Owner will receive the following royalties for each original episode produced and broadcast (within ten [10] days after completion of each episode).

(i) For each program of up to and thirty (30) minutes in length, Seven Hundred Fifty Dollars ($750); or

(ii) For each program in excess of thirty (30) minutes and up to and including sixty (60) minutes in length, One Thousand Dollars ($1,000); or

(iii) For each program in excess of sixty (60) and up to and including ninety (90) minutes in length, One Thousand Two Hundred Fifty Dollars ($1,250).

Twenty percent (20%) of the applicable series royalty will be payable for each of the first five U.S. reruns of each episode. No further sums will be payable for any other runs of such episode. Initial run royalty payments shall be made upon commencement of production of the program involved. Rerun payments shall be paid within sixty (60) days after the broadcast triggering payment. If such episodic television series is broadcast more frequently than one program per week (e.g., a daytime serial), the applicable per program royalty set forth above shall constitute payment for each full week of programming.

(e) In the event a spin-off of the television series referenced above (excluding a "miniseries," "movie-of-the-week" or the Picture itself) is produced by Producer based on said series and Owner is not engaged to render writing or other services in connection therewith, Owner will receive fifty percent (50%) of the applicable network royalties specified above for "generic" spin-off series and twenty-five percent (25%) of the applicable network royalties specified above for "planted" spin-off series.

(f) In the event any television production referenced in subparagraph (c), (d) or (e) above is initially produced for U.S. non–prime time or U.S. non-network broadcast, Owner shall be entitled to an amount equal to fifty percent (50%) of the applicable royalty set forth in said paragraph.

In the event Purchaser shall fail to make any of the aforesaid payments within the time and in the manner hereinabove set forth, Owner acknowledges and agrees that Owner's sole remedy shall be an action at law to recover such payments, and in no event shall any of said rights revert to Owner, nor shall Owner have or be deemed to have any lien, charge or other encumbrance upon said rights to secure payment of said sums.

Note that probably you will not be entitled to receive a passive payment if you happen to *write* the particular production for which you would otherwise receive a passive payment. The reason: You will probably receive a lot more money to write a sequel or other subsequent production than the passive payments would amount to (as a rule, sequels and other subsequent productions are only produced if the first picture was a hit), and the studio does not want to pay you twice.

M. FIRST NEGOTIATION TO WRITE A SEQUEL OR OTHER SUBSEQUENT PRODUCTION

Odds are that if the first picture is a huge hit and you wrote it, the studio will want you back to write a sequel at a much higher price. Still, studios do have their pet writers and you may be aced out if you do not negotiate some protection for yourself in this arena. It is quite common to negotiate a right of first negotiation to write a sequel, remake or other subsequent production. And if the first production was a feature, for example, the studio will agree that your price on a sequel picture will not be lower than the salary you received on the first picture.

Whether you sell a script or you are commissioned to write it, your opportunity to write a sequel will most certainly be based on your having received sole "screenplay by" or sole "written by" credit on the first picture *and* sole separated rights. (The Writers Guild awards "written by" credit if no other writer wrote the story, "screenplay by" credit if there is a separate story writer.) The studio's argument is that if other writers have to be brought in on the first picture, the picture consists of material that is no longer just your material (in their mind, your material was not good enough to make a picture) and thus they insist on these conditions. Remember, if a picture is produced based on your original story and characters—unless a subsequent writer changes the essential elements dramatically —you will most probably be awarded sole separated rights. Given Hollywood's tradition of using many writers on a project, you may not receive sole screenplay credit. Thus, unfortunately, you can easily lose your right to write subsequent productions. This is usually not negotiable.

What if your screenplay is based on a book or other source material? Let's say that you do receive sole "screenplay by" credit on the first picture. You will not receive sole separated rights unless you also wrote the book, and thus you may not get the opportunity to write a sequel. In such cases, I try to negotiate for the writer the right to write a sequel if he/she gets sole "screenplay by" credit. Separated rights should not be an issue, because the book writer will not be asked to write a sequel to the movie. So why should the studio care? Some studios accept this argument, most do not, which I think is unfair. Keep in mind that if the first picture is a big hit and you did receive sole "screenplay by" credit, you will probably get the right to write the sequel anyway, so it is not worth breaking a deal over.

What if the first picture is a big hit and then becomes a television series? You should also try to get the right to write the pilot script (the prototype episode for the series). If you do, though, your right will always be subject to network approval, and unless you have written for television and, in particular, a pilot script, you may not get the shot. Networks tend to favor, and desire, experienced writers of television series to write their pilot scripts. It is a barrier that is extremely difficult to cross.

N. GUARANTEED REWRITES AND WRITING ASSIGNMENTS: WHEN YOU SELL A SPEC SCREENPLAY OR A BOOK

Your philosophy, of course, is to stay with the project as long as you can. If you have optioned or sold an original script to a producer, you want the opportunity to write at least one rewrite and, moreover, the opportunity to do that rewrite before any other writer is hired. Under the current WGA rules, the producer must offer the writer the first rewrite. This was a major breakthrough in the 1988 collective bargaining negotiation between the producers and the Writers Guild. It was a long time coming.

Article 16.A.3c of the WGA Basic Agreement provides that:

. . . with respect to a screenplay sold or licensed to Company (i.e., the studio or producer) by a "professional writer" who is awarded separated rights *[see discussion above],* the Company shall offer the first writer the opportunity to perform the first rewrite services at not less than the applicable minimum compensation for a rewrite. If such writer is unable to perform such services or waives his/her right, the Company may engage another writer.

In addition, the Company shall offer such writer the opportunity to perform one (1) additional set of revisions, if they are required by the Company, because of a changed or new element (e.g., director or principal performer) assigned to the development or production of the writer's screenplay. The Company's obligation to make such an offer shall exist for a period of two years after delivery of the writer's first or final set of revisions, whichever occurs later. *However,* this obligation does not arise if the Company engaged another writer to make revisions to the screenplay before the first changed or new element was assigned to the project. If the first writer is unable to perform such services or waives his/her right, the Company may engage another writer.

Even if you are not a WGA member, you should still insist on the guaranteed opportunity to write the first rewrite. After all, it is your script that someone else is tinkering with. You should have the first crack at rewriting it. It is crucial. Once you have optioned or sold your script to someone else, they own it. They control it. In their minds and in accordance with Hollywood tradition, they can do whatever they want with it.

Luckily, today, few producers will object. Since this provision was added to the WGA Agreement, it has become an accepted norm of the business. If a producer does object, then you should suspect his intentions—obviously, the producer intends to kick you off the project as soon as that producer gains control of the material. Confront him or her. If the producer does not back down, think twice about that deal.

Note that under the Guild rule, you are only guaranteed WGA minimum for a rewrite, which in 1994–1995 is $12,569 for a low budget picture (under $2,500,000) or $18,978 for a high budget picture (over $2,500,000). You should try to negotiate a higher fee. If you have been paid $100,000 for a first draft, it is ridiculous to accept $18,978 for a rewrite. Between $25,000 and $50,000 would be more appropriate. Depending on your leverage and how much you may have been paid in the past for a rewrite (studios always ask for previous quotes), you will be able to increase your rewrite guarantee above the minimum compensation dictated by the Guild.

Most agreements that combine the option/purchase of a spec screenplay with writing services also provide that the payment for writing services is applicable against the purchase of the screenplay. Thus if your script is optioned to a third-party producer and you are asked to render writing services, your writing compensation (not including pension, health and welfare payments made on your behalf to the Writers Guild) will be deducted from the purchase price when the option is exercised. As an example, your script is under option. You are asked to write a rewrite and a polish and are paid for such. You receive $35,000 for your writing services. The purchase price is $300,000. There were two $5,000 option payments, one non-applicable. At the time of purchase, you will receive $300,000, less $5,000 for the applicable option payment, less $35,000 for the writing services, or a total of $260,000. When a script is purchased outright, the buyer might also require writing services as part of the compensation. A young client of mine recently sold his screenplay for $300,000. The agreement provided that the buyer could require him to render unlimited writing services. We tried to negotiate for a limit on such services (e.g., three rewrites tops). The studio would not budge, and ultimately, the writer accepted the deal. The studio maintains that the script is close to a shooting script. We'll see. (Note that the Writers Guild imposes certain limitations on unlimited rewriting. As a rule of thumb if the compensation on a weekly basis doesn't at least add up to $3,000 per week, the studio can't ask for more writing, i.e., if you are getting $30,000 for 10 weeks of work, the studio can't ask you to write for 11 weeks.)

O. "DEAD SCREENPLAY" PROBLEM

There is one downside to your obtaining the right to do rewrites on scripts that you option to a studio or a producer. It is a critical problem that you need to be aware of. The reality in Hollywood is that very few screenplays which are optioned actually get purchased and/or made. I do not know if anyone could tell you an exact percentage, but it is fairly low. Given that reality, the question you should be asking yourself is "What happens to my rewrite if my script is only optioned and not purchased?" Remember that writing services fall under the category of a "work made for hire" (see Chapter Two above). In other words, the person who pays for it owns it. Thus, if your script is optioned but it is not purchased (i.e., the option expires), you get your original script back, but the person who commissioned the rewrite owns the rewrite!

Suppose this happens to you: An option expires and now you want to option your screenplay to someone else. You can only option the original screenplay without the rewrite (or anyone else's rewrite, for that matter) and all the good work that you put into that rewrite. Remember, someone else owns it and you cannot touch it—any of it, except those portions which existed in the original screenplay. If you do use any of the rewritten material, you or whoever uses the rewrite can be sued for copyright infringement by the owner of the rewrite. The studio owns that material and the copyright in that material. You will also be sued by the second buyer of your script if you do not disclose the fact that someone else owns a rewrite. As you will note later in this book (under Chapter Three R, concerning representation and warranties), one of the warranties that a writer must make to the buyer of his material is that the writer owns that material. If not, the writer has breached that provision of the contract and could be denied certain entitlements (i.e., monies) under that contract.

There is one solution to this problem. You can ask for a *reversion* of your rewrite(s) if your script is optioned, but not purchased. In other words, when the option expires, the rights to your rewrite are assigned to you. You will control it and may sell it again. If you are lucky enough to get a reversion clause, you may have to, and you probably will have to, agree to pay back the cost of the rewrite when and if the picture gets made. More likely, you will probably be asked to (1) pay back all costs that the buyer has incurred in connection with the project instead of just rewrite costs (in this case, try to limit it to actual costs—without overhead or interest) and (2) to pay back the costs *when you set the project up* with someone else. Keep in mind that you will not actually pay these costs. The buyer of your material will have to pay. It may be a deterrent for the buyer but if he/she wants it badly enough, then at least you have the opportunity to make a deal.

What if the payback cost is too high? Will that prevent you from ever selling or optioning your script again? It should not. If the costs are too high, then the next buyer can try to renegotiate with the owner of the rewrite(s) at the time the next buyer comes on board. Particularly if the financier/producer that paid for the rewrite is a studio and the next buyer is a studio. Studios sometimes have reciprocal arrangements between themselves that allow for discounts or payments over time. Each studio at some point is a buyer and a seller, so it is to their mutual advantage to work out arrangements that are good for each of them. At least if you get a reversion, you will have *control* of your rewrites and will be able to sell them, which may be essential depending how much material you may have added.

The problem, and it is getting worse, is that many of the major studios will not agree to reversions. (See discussion in Section E above.) They want to hold on to their rewrite(s). They say, "Trust us. Approach us when someone else is interested and we will be happy to talk to them." Should you be concerned? On the one hand, one can argue that a rewrite without the underlying material is of no value to a studio. They cannot do anything with it. On the other hand, remember, studios are competitors and they may not want to make it easy for their rival to make use of the extra material that they developed. The point is that without a reversion, you have no control over the situation. Note that if the studio will not agree to give you a reversion in your rewrite, then this rewrite becomes what is called a "dead screenplay"—dead because you cannot do anything with it.

Some argue that the studio attitude about reversions of rewritten material creates an incentive for a writer to hold back his best thoughts until he knows the picture is going to be made and *his screenplay bought.* In other words, if commissioned to do a rewrite during an option period, the writer will do what the studio tells him to do, but will not introduce his best ideas in case the project does not get made at that studio, so that he can use these ideas later on. Unfortunately, the studio attitude encourages this behavior and I think it is outrageous that reversions are not automatic. Studios should give them. Let the negotiations be about the payback provision (e.g., whether interest should be charged on costs, whether all costs incurred should be paid back or just the cost of the rewrite). At least give the writer the chance to move on if the project is ultimately discarded by the first studio. As noted, odds are it will be.

This same philosophy should be applied for screenplays that are purchased outright from the writer. At some point, they should revert; otherwise, the screenplay might sit on the shelf and if the studio will not give the writer a reversion, again it is "dead."

While it is true that the entertainment business is a business, it is also true that writers are not in it just for the money. It is important that they get their projects made. Thankfully, the WGA has finally succeeded in introducing a provision that grants writers the right to buy back their material after a certain period of time (see discussion above). While there are drawbacks to the Guild rule (mainly the time periods—the right may not kick in for many years after an option has expired), at least it creates an opportunity for the writer to get around the potentially devastating "dead screenplay" problem.

Most writers are forced to accept the fact that they will not have the ability to buy back their rewrites, except pursuant to the WGA rules, and that if someone is interested enough in their material, that person will, hopefully, work it out with the owner of the rewrite and make a deal. In short, be aware of the problem and in all cases try to get a reversion of your material. Insist on it if it is an independent producer or a small company. Ask for it at a major studio and, if you cannot get it, decide whether you are willing to take the risk or break a deal, keeping in mind all of the factors—pros and cons—that I have outlined above. The reality is that writers are constantly forced to make deals in light of the studio mentality toward them, which in many respects can be patently unfair. This is just one more example.

P. YOUR GOAL: A GUARANTEE TO WRITE
—AND TO WRITE BEFORE ANYONE ELSE GETS A CHANCE

The goal of most writers is to stay with the project as long as possible. Contractually, this is called a "guarantee." You are guaranteed the right to write a certain number of drafts. (The guarantee is discussed more in detail in the next chapter, about writing assignments.)

The WGA provision that guarantees the writer of a spec screenplay one rewrite under certain circumstances (discussed above in Section N), also guarantees the writer the opportunity to do that rewrite *before* the company can engage the services of another writer. Even if you are not a Guild member, you should try to get this same right. In other words, the contract should explicitly stipulate that the studio/producer may not engage the services of another writer until you have turned in your rewrite.

What if you are guaranteed several steps? As an example, a rewrite and a polish. Ideally, you want to stay on the project for both drafts until any other writer is brought on board. As you know, the impulse in Hollywood is to hire another writer if the script is not perfect. You have to negotiate your rights. My view is that if the employer is stuck paying you for another draft, they will probably ask for it and then, of course, look at it. And if they like it, then their interest in you might very well be renewed. It just works that way. This part of your negotiation is therefore very important. At the very least the employer should agree not to hire another writer until after you have turned in your *first* guaranteed step, although most studios will not put this in the contract.

Note that many studios agree to hire the writer for the first rewrite with the right to "cut off" any further writing steps after that point. Invariably, they will want an option for further writing steps. Remember, that any such right is an option only, for the studio's purpose. It guarantees you nothing. As discussed in more detail in the next chapter, when the employer delays a writing step, you should still receive your guaranteed payment as if the postponement never occurred.

Q. BOOKS SPECIFICALLY

Agreements for the option and sale of books are similar to those for screenplays. I have already discussed some of these similarities above. Recall that with books, it is essential and customary for the author to reserve all publication rights. It is also easier to negotiate a reversion should a picture not be produced within a certain period of time. There are several other differences.

For one, if the book is optioned prior to publication, you may want to provide for a bonus should the book be a success. Such bonuses are normally payable only if the option is exercised, and are generally tied to *The New York Times* bestseller list. The norm is that you will receive a payment for each week that the book is #1 on the list, a lower payment for each week that the book is #2 though #4 on the list and a still lower payment for each week that the book is #5 through #10 on the list.

Secondly, you will be required to have the publisher of your book sign a "publisher's release." This is a statement by the publisher that it does not own any motion picture, television or other allied rights in the book. Publishers are accustomed to signing such releases. Here is a sample of such release:

PUBLISHER'S RELEASE

For good and valuable consideration, receipt of which is hereby acknowledged, the undersigned hereby acknowledges and agrees for the express benefit of Big Studio Films ("Purchaser"), and Purchaser's successors, licensees and assigns, in perpetuity throughout the universe, that the undersigned has no claim to or interest in the motion picture, television and allied and incidentary rights or any other rights of any other kind whatsoever other than print publication rights which have been heretofore granted to the undersigned in or to that certain literary work (the "Property") published by the undersigned and described as follows:

Title: *The Hot Book*
Written by: [Your Name]
Copyright
Registration:

The undersigned hereby consents insofar as it is concerned to the publication and copyright by and/or in the name of Purchaser, or its successors, licensees and assigns, in any and all languages; throughout the universe, in any form or media, (i) synopses, dramatizations, abridged and/or revised versions of, or excerpts from, the Property, not exceeding 10,000 words each and to be serialized, adapted or extracted from the Property or from any motion picture and/or other version of the Property for the purpose of advertising, publicizing and/or promotion any such motion picture and/or other version, or (ii) screenplays, so-called "photonovels" consisting of still photographs from any motion picture produced based on the Property with captions or other written material, so-called "making of" publications.

IN WITNESS WHEREOF, the undersigned has executed this instrument this _____ day of _____, 199_____.

By: _____

Its: _____

If you are a book writer, you are probably aware that even though you have created the characters, the plot and everything else, in Hollywood's eyes you are probably not qualified to write a screenplay. Of course, you do have leverage. You do not have to sell the rights to your book without being afforded the right to write the screenplay.

If you are given the opportunity to write a screenplay, the question then becomes, how many drafts will you be allowed to write? If you are fortunate, one draft and a rewrite. That is the most usually given. And remember, even if you get that right, it is not uncommon for producers to start again from scratch. They may throw out all of your material.

If you have never written a screenplay, then, for the most part, about all you can expect is minimum compensation to write the screenplay. When we say "minimum" in Hollywood, that usually means WGA minimum, the minimum payment required by the Writers Guild of America for the particular work you are asked to write. For a first draft and a set of revisions, for 1994 (5/1/94–5/1/95), for a low budget film (under $2,500,000), the minimum is $20,947. For a high budget picture (over $2,500,000), the minimum is $43,106. Make sure that this payment is over and above the monies you will receive for your book. In other words, the screenwriting monies are not applicable in any way to the book monies.

If the producer you are dealing with agrees to your writing the screenplay, keep in mind that most producers will certainly ask for something in return, such as a low option price on the book for the opportunity they are giving you to be hired to write the screenplay. That is not a bad position to be in.

The next question then becomes, *when* will you be hired? Commonly, the producer will agree to hire you if anyone is hired to write a screenplay. In such case, you will be hired before anyone else has a chance. That works in your favor if the producer intends to hire a writer upon commencement of the option. If the producer is looking for a studio to finance the writing services, then you will have to wait until he/she sets up the project at a studio. Most producers are unwilling to pay for writing services without the backing of a financier, even if you are a seasoned screenwriter. It is a critical reality of the business. In that case, you have no way of knowing when, if ever, your services will commence.

Odds are that the studio will want a script written as soon as the studio makes its deal with the producer (studios are in the film business and generally don't option books unless they intend to develop them. The cases are rare today that a studio will option a book just to take it off the market). More importantly, odds are, too, that the producer is also looking to a studio to finance the option payment for the book and may even have made a deal with the studio with respect to that book before the producer closes the book deal with the writer. In my opinion, if you are interested in writing the screenplay, and the producer agrees to give you that right, you should take the deal even if the project has not yet been set up. That is, if you believe in the producer's abilities. But if you are concerned that you may never get the chance to write, ask the producer if he is financing the writing of the screenplay himself or if he has already presented the book to a studio. That way, you will know before signing the deal your chances of your actually writing the screenplay.

R. REPRESENTATIONS AND WARRANTIES

If you sell or option a spec screenplay or a book, and even when you are commissioned to write, you will be required to make certain representations and warranties concerning your work. These "reps and warranties," as they are commonly referred to, are crucial to the studio. Here is an example of a typical reps and warranties provision:

1. *WARRANTIES:* Owner represents, warrants and agrees:

(a) That Owner is the sole owner of all rights herein granted and has full power and authority to grant said rights to Purchaser, as more particularly set forth in this agreement, and to agree to the restrictions upon the exercise of the rights reserved to Owner, as more particularly set forth in this agreement; that none of said rights have been granted, encumbered or otherwise disposed of in any manner to any person; that no motion picture based in whole or in part upon the Work has been produced or authorized by or with the knowledge or consent of Owner; that neither the Work nor any version thereof nor any play or dramatic adaptation based thereon in whole or in part have been published or presented or authorized on television, radio or on the spoken stage by or with the knowledge or consent of Owner;

that Owner has not done or omitted to do and will not do or omit to do any act or thing, by license, grant or otherwise, which will or may impair or encumber any of the rights herein granted or interfere with the full enjoyment of said rights; and that there are no claims or litigation pending or threatened which will or might adversely affect any of the rights herein granted to Purchaser.

(b) That the Work is original with Owner; that neither the Work nor any part thereof is taken from or based upon any other material or any motion picture; and that neither the Work nor any part thereof, or the exercise by Purchaser of any of the rights herein granted, will violate or infringe upon the trademark, trade name, copyright, patent, literary, dramatic, musical, artistic, personal, private, civil or property right or, to the best of Owner's knowledge, right of privacy or publicity or constitute a libel or slander of any person.

(c) That the Work is not in the public domain and enjoys, and will enjoy, either statutory or common law copyright protection in the United States and all countries adhering to the Berne and Universal Copyright Conventions; and that the rights granted to Purchaser hereunder are and will be exclusive.

Owner will defend, indemnify, make good, save and hold harmless Purchaser, its successors and assigns, from and against any liability, losses, claims, damages, costs, charges, reasonable attorneys' fees, recoveries, actions, judgments, penalties, expenses and other loss whatsoever, which may be obtained against, imposed upon or suffered by Purchaser, its successors and assigns by reason of the use of the Work by Purchaser, its successors or assigns, or the breach of any warranty, covenant, agreement or representation herein made by Owner. Purchaser shall indemnify and hold Owner harmless against any and all liability, losses, claims, damages, costs, charges, reasonable attorneys' fees, recoveries, actions, judgments, penalties, expenses and other loss arising out of or in connection with any assigned material or material added by Purchaser to the Work except to the extent any such liability results from a breach of Owner's representations, warranties or agreements hereunder.

Basically, the studio wants to know that, claim free, it will obtain good title to your material. Just like with the sale of a house or a car, the studio must be assured that you own the rights that you are selling and that no one else is going to claim ownership in that material. The studio also wants to know that your work is original with you and that you haven't worked with another writer on it or, if you have, that you have disclosed it. They also want to be assured that your material is not based on an actual person's life story, in which case they would need releases from that person.

You should know that under Article 28 of the Writers Guild Agreement, the Guild insists that any warranties concerning material which may be based on actual persons be "to the best of the writer's knowledge" only. These warranties are the ones contained in subparagraph (b) above concerning rights of privacy, publicity, libel and slander. In other words, you will not be required to say absolutely that your characters do not resemble actual persons. Rather, to the best of your knowledge, your characters are not based on actual persons and you are not aware of infringing any other person's personal rights. The Writers Guild has recognized that writers are not lawyers and that writers often create material which is based on personal experience and personal relationships. In that sense, you are likely to draw from your own experience and use incidents that have happened between you and other persons. While you will probably not depict those other persons' lives as the core of your material, you may use an event, a meeting, an encounter with that real person in your material and the depiction of your own fictional character.

The other reason that the Writers Guild limits representations concerning libel, slander, rights of privacy and publicity to the best of the writer's knowledge is that the Writers Guild recognizes that there may be someone in the world who might try to *claim* that one of your characters resembles that person's character and that your plot resembles that person's life story. And, indeed, there are often "nuisance suits" if a picture is successful—someone trying to make a buck by filing a lawsuit. Even if you are not a member of the Guild, you should insist that your contract contain the same "to the best of your knowledge" qualification as set forth in Article 28 of the WGA Basic Agreement and that you are covered on the errors and omissions policy (see discussion below). You should not be blamed for, or be liable for, nuisance suits.

For your reference, Article 28 states:

ARTICLE 28: WARRANTY AND INDEMNIFICATION (GENERAL)

1. Company and writer may in any individual contract of employment include provisions for warranties of originality and no violation of rights of third parties, indemnification against judgments, damages, costs and expenses including attorneys' fees in connection with suits relating to the literary material or the use of the literary material supplied by the writer or the use thereof by Company; provided, however, that the writer shall in no event

(a) be required by contract to waive his/her right to defend himself/herself against a claim by Company for costs, damages or losses arising out of settlements not consented to by the writer; and Company reserves all of the rights it may otherwise have against the writer;

(b) be required to warrant or indemnify with respect to any claims that his/her literary material defamed or invaded the privacy of any person *unless the writer knowingly used the name or personality of such person or should have known, in the exercise of reasonable prudence, that such person would or might claim that his/her personality was used in such material;*

(c) be required to warrant or indemnify with respect to any material other than that furnished by the writer;

(d) be required to warrant or indemnify with respect to third party defamation, invasion of privacy or publicity claims, where the writer is requested by the Company to prepare literary materials which are based in whole or in part on any actual individual, whether living or dead, provided writer accurately provides all information reasonably requested by Company for the purpose of permitting the Company to evaluate the risks involved in the utilization of the material supplied by writer.

Contracts are often drafted in the following manner to reflect the provisions contained in Article 28:

Owner represents and warrants that the Work is original with Owner; that neither the Work nor any part thereof is taken from or based upon any other material or any motion picture; and that neither the Work nor any part thereof, nor the exercise by Purchaser of any of the rights herein granted, will violate or infringe upon the trademark, trade name, copyright, patent, literary, dramatic, musical, artistic, personal, private, civil or property right, *or to the best of Owner's knowledge,* right of privacy or any other right of any person or constitute a libel or slander of any person.

Assuming that you created your material independently and are not in breach of any of your representations and warranties, what do you do if there is a lawsuit against the studio concerning your material or any additions which may be made to it by the studio? Will you be sued? Odds are you will be named. Does that mean you run the risk of spending thousands of dollars on legal costs by virtue of your being in business with a powerful, rich third party? Is the risk worth it?

Rest easy: studios and producers are able to protect themselves against many of these claims by obtaining insurance. This insurance is called "errors and omissions insurance," and is commonly referred to as "E & O insurance." Basically, this insurance covers claims of similarity, such as claims of copyright infringement and idea similarity. It also covers claims by persons who assert that the material in question is about their own life story—i.e., the plot in the story is that person's own life story, or a character in the screenplay has the same character traits as that person. Nuisance suits and copyright infringement suits are covered by the insurance company to the extent that the studio and you are not actually guilty of infringement. The insurance company also assumes innocence and unless they can prove that knowledgeable infringement has occurred, they will cover the damages over and above the deductible. Yes, just like any other insurance policy, there is usually a deductible—$10,000 to $15,000 for each claim. While contracts do not state specifically that the studio will cover the deductible, it is an unwritten common policy for the studio or for the producer to do so, and I do not know of any instance in which the writer has been asked to contribute. Policy limits are generally $1 million for each occurrence ($3 million aggregate coverage on any one picture), although in recent years these amounts have increased to $3 million for each occurrence ($5 million aggregate coverage on any one picture). Most claims are settled out of court.

What you need is to be certain you are covered by the insurance policy. Indeed, the Writers Guild Basic Agreement requires that "the Company shall name or cover the writer . . . as an *additional insured* on its errors and omissions policies respecting theatrical and television motion pictures."

In addition, the Basic Agreement states that "the Company shall indemnify such writer against any and all damages, costs and expenses, including attorneys' fees, and shall relieve the writer of all liability in connection with any claim or action respecting material supplied to the writer by the Company for incorporation into the writer's work or incorporated into the writer's work by employees or officers of the Company other than the writer." This indemnity is often referred to as a "reciprocal indemnity"—reciprocal because the writer also gives in indemnity regarding his own material (as discussed above).

Even though these provisions exist in the Guild Agreement, I always ask that the contract specifically spell out the protections embodied in these two provisions. (Note also that the WGA provisions do not apply to all writers. Animation writers, as an example, are not covered by the WGA.) It is common practice in the industry to do so and it is also important for the writer making his own representations and warranties to see in the contract that he/she will be protected. I also try to embellish the provision concerning added material to include changes made to the writer's material (a change, such as a deletion, may not necessarily be construed as an addition). Bottom line, what this means is that (1) the studio will cover the costs of any lawsuits that the writer is named in resulting from material that is not the writer's and that may be included in the final screenplay or motion picture, and (2) an insurance policy will cover material that is the writer's as long as the writer has not knowingly infringed someone else's rights.

Here is an example of the provision:

Purchaser shall indemnify and hold Owner harmless against any and all liability, losses, claims, damages, costs, charges, reasonable attorneys' fees, recoveries, actions, judgments, penalties, expenses and other loss arising out of or in connection with any assigned material or material added by Purchaser to the Work, except to the extent any such liability results from a breach or alleged breach of Owner's representation, warranties or agreements hereunder. Purchaser agrees that Owner shall be covered as an additional insured under the errors and omissions policy in connection with the Picture to the extent Purchaser has obtained errors and omissions insurance for the Picture.

There is one pitfall which you need to be aware of. The WGA Agreement refers to the fact that the company must cover the writer under its policy. Suppose it does not have a policy? The word *its* is ambiguous in this context, and arguably, if the company has no policy, it does not have to list the writer as an additional insured. I therefore ask that the writer be named on *an* errors and omissions policy. If the company does not take one out, then they are in breach and they will have to cover you. The reciprocal indemnity also ensures the company's obligations to you.

If you are not a member of the Writers Guild, then you must ask for these provisions and make sure that the company agrees to list you as an *additional* insured on their coverage. It is a minimum incremental cost for the studio, and they should send you a certificate indicating that you have been covered.

S. INDEMNIFICATION: BREACH VERSUS ALLEGED BREACH

Look carefully at the last paragraph of the reps and warranties provision that I quoted in Section R above. Notice that you are requested to indemnify the studio if you have breached (violated) your reps and warranties. Your indemnity requires you to pay for the damages incurred by the studio as a result of your failure to live up to your reps and warranties, including lawyers' fees and court costs. On a successful motion picture, needless to say, the damages could be extremely high! The studio holds you accountable in these critical areas.

Most contracts in their initial draft state that the writer must indemnify the studio for a "breach" or "alleged breach" of that writer's representations, warranties and agreements under that contract. It is important to understand the distinction between these two terms.

If the writer has "breached" his/her contract, that means that the writer has basically failed to comply with his/her obligations under that contract. This is also called "default." For instance, the writer may have stated that he wrote his material alone when, in fact, he wrote with a writing partner. The writer may have actually based his/her material on a true story without disclosing this fact. The writer may have violated any of the other reps and warranties or any other promise contained in the writer's contract. If the writer is rendering services, the writer may have delivered material late. If you do breach—specifically, you take too long to write a draft, you write another project when your services are supposed to be exclusive, you are not available during a reading period, you disregard the studio's instructions regarding a rewrite (when asked to do a rewrite, the contract always provides that you must incorporate the studio's requests), you sell a screenplay that you do not own, you say you are the sole writer and someone else has helped you—then your contract automatically terminates certain benefits. Even if you are entitled to a screenplay credit, for instance, you may be denied your bonus. You may be denied your profits, denied the opportunity to write a sequel, and you may be denied your right to receive the passive payments that you negotiated.

An "alleged breach" is a *claim* that the writer has breached. In other words, a studio may claim that you have breached, but you can also say that you have not. Ultimately, if there is a dispute as to which side is right, it is up to a court to decide. That is expensive. And even if you win, remember that lawyers' fees are not automatically awarded to the prevailing party, so you might find yourself having to pay them yourself.

The main reason to focus on the distinction between

breach and *alleged breach* is that if you can be denied compensation for an alleged breach, you can be denied compensation if the studio *says* you have not complied. That is enough to deny you your rights—most importantly, your compensation. Lawyers in Hollywood always ask to have this provision deleted, and often the studios will delete it. The contract will then say that you must have breached your contract in order for there to be the right to deny you your rights, which means that the *burden* is on the *studio* to *prove* that you breached. Unfortunately, taking out the "alleged breach" language does not mean that the studio will not try to claim you breached before it has been proven and stop paying you your money. You may have to sue anyway. At the very least, though, the consensus in Hollywood is that by deleting the "alleged breach" language, it does mean that the studio will not be able to claim breach without having *strong* grounds to do so.

Fortunately, most writers do not breach their contracts and if they need more time to write a particular draft, for instance, the studio will listen. Make sure, if the studio agrees to give you more time to write a screenplay, to confirm this point in writing. If the studio has agreed to it, then technically it is not a breach, but you will want to make sure that you have a record of it. The consequences of breaching a contract can be costly and you do not want to take any chances.

Finally, in defining what is a breach or default, lawyers always make the point that the breach or default must be a "material" one in order for you to be denied your rights. You will often see language such as "provided writer has not *materially* breached his obligations hereunder . . ." If you deliver the screenplay a half hour late, in most circumstances, that will not be considered "material,'' so you should not be denied your compensation or other perks.

T. CREDITS

The Writers Guild determines credits through formal procedures. Before the credits for a film or television program are placed on the screen, the company which has produced a show must submit its proposed credits to the Guild. This notice is sent to all writers (Guild and non-Guild) who have written any material in connection with that program. If the writer protests the proposed credits, he/she may object, in which case the Guild will arbitrate a decision.

Note that in the case of a dispute, the Guild, Theatrical Schedule A.7, allows all participating writers to reach a compromise among themselves. Beware of this provision, however. Most studio contracts which provide bonuses to writers based on screenplay credit *disallow* the bonus if the writers decide among themselves how the credits should be finalized. The reason: One writer may get a very high bonus for a sole credit. He could conceivably make a side deal with the other writers to split his compensation for sole screenplay credit, which in the end may earn *all* writers more money than if they had not made such a deal. That is why the following language appears in contracts in respect of screenplay bonuses: "If the writer is awarded sole screenplay credit (other than pursuant to Theatrical Schedule A of the WGA Basic Agreement), then he/she shall receive . . .''

In an arbitration, three arbitrators are mutually selected to read all drafts of a work. The writer who disputes a proposed credit is requested to write a detailed analysis of why he is entitled to screenplay credit. Non-producer and non-director writers must contribute at least 33% of the final screenplay to receive credit. The requirement for producer/writers or director/writers (called "hyphenates" in Hollywood) is more stringent. Hyphenates must contribute at least 50% to get credit.

To give you an idea of how the credit arbitration works, here is an example. A producer optioned a screenplay. The first writer was required to do a rewrite. The director insisted on another rewrite, but did not want to use the original screenplay writer. The producer wrote a rewrite. In the credit arbitration, the producer's name was submitted as the screenplay writer and the names of the two persons who had created the story were submitted as the story writers (these two writers had not written the original screenplay, only the story). The original screenplay writer protested (remember, his material was based on original story material). Because the producer was a hyphenate, he needed to contribute 50% of the screenplay material. The first arbitration awarded the producer sole screenplay credit, with story by the original story writers. The original screenwriter protested again. (Under certain very limited circumstances, one may reexamine an arbitration. In this case, the screenwriter stated to the Guild that they had not examined all of the facts.) Indeed, they had not and final screenplay credits were awarded to the producer *and* the original *story* writers as having written the screenplay, with story by the original story writers. The protesting screenwriter had lost this second round as well. The original story was so extensive that it was deemed in part to be original screenplay material. Very little of the original screenwriter's dialogue or contributions remained. The producer did rely heavily on the story and the original story writers' contribution (which upon examination was closer to a screenplay than just a story), so the story writers were entitled to screenplay credit as well.

The advantage of the WGA credit arbitration is that it is free for the writers and the producers. It is a service of the Guild and a very valuable one.

CHAPTER FOUR

WRITING ASSIGNMENTS

A. SERVICES

1. Exclusivity

Almost all writing services agreements contain the requirement that the writer's services must be exclusive during the period that the writer is writing. The studio is paying for your services and they want to ensure that your services are wholly devoted to the material that they are commissioning. Barring extenuating circumstances, the studio expects to receive the material which they have commissioned at the time stipulated in your contract. That is not to say that they will not give you more time. If the reason is that you are working on another project, however, they may not. The so-called reading periods which follow delivery of each step of the writing process (e.g., after delivery of the first draft, rewrite and polish, and so on) require the writer to be non-exclusive. That is the period for the producer to review the material, talk to you about it and talk to whomever he needs to talk to (e.g., studio brass) before going to the next step.

2. Guaranteed Steps

If you are commissioned to write a screenplay, you will usually be commissioned for a first draft and a rewrite, and, sometimes, a polish (although the polish is usually optional). The non-optional commitments are called the "guarantee" and you are guaranteed the negotiated compensation for those steps.

Writers usually get ten to twelve weeks to turn in a first draft and another four to six weeks for a rewrite. The polish writing period is two to four weeks. Reading periods are usually four weeks. What this means is that once you have committed to write, you cannot take on any other assignments until you finish the guaranteed steps. Thus, if you are commissioned for a first draft screenplay and rewrite and the writing periods are ten weeks and four weeks respectively, you may not take another writing assignment for ten weeks (first draft) + four weeks (reading period) + four weeks (rewrite) for a total of eighteen weeks. (If you are a Writers Guild member, there is a limit to the number of weeks that a producer may employ you, which depends on your level of compensation. See discussion below in subchapter A.4.)

Almost all studios pay one half the required compensation on commencement of services for the particular draft and one half on delivery. Suppose you are paid $60,000 for a first draft and a rewrite. Forty thousand is allocated to the first draft and $20,000 is allocated to the rewrite. You will be paid $20,000 on commencement of the first draft, $20,000 on delivery of the first draft, $10,000 on commencement of the rewrite and $20,000 on delivery of the rewrite.

3. Postponement

The studio may decide to postpone the second step after the reading period, or the third step, and so on. In that case, you should be able to take other assignments. Studios usually do have the option to postpone the second or third guaranteed step, in which case you will still have to render the applicable services at later date, but they will be subject to your professional availability. There are two points to be negotiated in this regard. First, if the studio postpones a step you should still get paid for that step *as if* the step had not been postponed. Thus, using the example above, if you were supposed to have started the rewrite after fourteen weeks but it is postponed, you would still be paid your commencement money for the rewrite in the fourteenth week and your delivery money in the eighteenth week. (Remember, you were given four weeks to write it.)

The second point you can try to negotiate is a limitation on the amount of time the studio has to postpone your services. Some studios will give a limitation of one year, some two years. Thus, if a writing step is postponed, the studio cannot ask you to write that step later than one or two years past the date on which they decided to postpone the step. Of course, if you are unavailable to write during that entire period, the period will be extended for the period of your unavailability.

4. Maximum Writing Time: Writers Guild Limitations

The Writers Guild Agreement provides for a minimum weekly writing salary for writers employed by the week. For 1994 (5/1/94–5/1/95) the amount is $3,088 for writers of feature films. Suppose the studio wants you to write a first draft screenplay for $30,000. You want fourteen weeks to write it. Technically, they cannot give you fourteen weeks. Fourteen times the minimum weekly amount exceeds $30,000. The studio must employ you for less than ten weeks for $30,000, so contractually you will not be able to write for fourteen weeks if you are a WGA member. Even if you are not a member of the Writers Guild, most studios are signatories to the Guild, so they are bound by Guild rules. Since this is a WGA requirement, studios are also loath to give you more than the maximum time allowed by the Guild, even noncontractually. If they knowingly allow you extra time to write, they expose themselves to a claim that you are entitled to extra compensation for the extra weeks worked, and they do not want to expose themselves to claims. That is not to say that extensions are never given. The studio has to trust that you will not raise the issue with the Guild. You probably think that if it is beneficial to the writer (in other words, you need the extra time and you do not care about the extra money), the Guild should not care. Believe me, they do. The WGA is a stickler regarding compliance with its rules. If they find out you are a member and you have violated WGA policy, they may fine you for non-compliance.

B. COMPENSATION

1. Guaranteed Payment

The most important part of any writer's deal is the up-front guarantee. How many drafts are you guaranteed: one draft, or one draft and rewrite, or one draft, one rewrite and one set of revisions? The more you write the better chance you have to get credit and, probably, a bonus. Most writing deals include a bonus for sole "screenplay by" credit and even shared "screenplay by" credit.

Ideally, if you are writing a first draft, you want a guaranteed rewrite and another polish. No one expects you to deliver a perfect first draft, so studios do not balk at giving you the added steps. They just try to keep the price down. Of course, if you are a Guild writer, there are limitations. The 1994 (5/1/94–5/1/95) minimum price for a treatment (which is a detailed outline of your screenplay—studios like to see this before you begin writing and they will pay extra for it), first draft and final draft screenplay (meaning revisions on your first draft) based on an original story is $37,938 for a low budget feature, $71,162 for a high budget picture, plus pension and welfare payments.

There is one drawback to being guaranteed too many steps. As mentioned above, you are under contract, *exclusive contract,* which means you cannot take other assignments. This could be particularly costly, for instance, if you were guaranteed one draft, one rewrite and four polishes. You get paid a fraction of the draft price for polishes ($6,226 for polishes for a low budget feature, $9,488 for a high budget). Compare this to the WGA's allocated amount for a draft screenplay of $14,941 for a low budget, $28,467 for a high budget first-draft screenplay. In other words, during all the time that you are polishing a script, you might have been hired to do a first draft screenplay on another script for almost three times the price of a polish. It is a big difference. Note, this is not a point to get hung up on. Studios usually will not guarantee four polishes anyway (remember that they want you to be disposable).

The more likely scenario is that the studio will require optional steps, meaning that if they like the first draft and the rewrite (remember, they tend to give you at least one shot to get it right), then they will want to keep you on. They also like to build in options at a set price. Optional services are almost always subject to your availability. (Unless, that is, they are ordered *immediately after* the guaranteed steps, in which case you have to remain available just as with a guarantee, but you are not guaranteed the assignment. This is slightly unfair, but optional steps are almost always postponed, and anyway, studios tend to be more flexible in this area, working around your availability.) In short, it is more than likely that you will be free to take on other assignments, so most writers plan on taking other assignments immediately after the guaranteed period is over. Studios usually need time to think, so odds are they will not ask for the optional steps right away. *Note:* When the studios talk about writing steps being subject to your availability, they mean "professional" availability. Personal unavailability does not count. You must be *contractually* bound to someone else.

2. Bonus Based on Credit

The other critical aspect of the employment deal is the bonus. Suppose you are the only writer on the project (rare, but it might happen). You get sole credit. You should be entitled to a bonus. Even if you get shared writing credit, you should get a bonus. Hollywood agrees. As I have mentioned, writers are basically disposable. However, if you stay on the project long enough and/or a sufficient amount of your work ends up in the final product, such that you get a shared credit or maybe a sole credit, the studio will give you a reward (see discussion below regarding credit determination). Most writers are able to negotiate a sole "screenplay by" credit bonus and a shared "screenplay by" credit bonus.

Writing deals are structured such that all of your guarantee and any additional monies you have been paid for optional steps are applied against the bonus. Thus, for example, if you negotiate a $175,000 sole "screenplay by" bonus and you have been paid $50,000 to write a draft and a set of revisions, you will receive $125,000 if you are awarded sole "screenplay by" credit.

The shared "screenplay by" bonus is usually one half of the difference between the amounts you have been paid and the sole "screenplay by" bonus. Thus, using the above example, your shared bonus would be $175,000 − $50,000 = $125,000/2 or $62,500. Some studios only give a flat fee for a shared bonus. If your deal is structured this way, the flat fee is usually a lower amount than you could make under the one-half sole "screenplay by" bonus formula. The flat rates would usually range between $25,000 and $50,000. Of course, it is negotiable. Top writers will receive more.

It is rare to see a "story by" credit bonus in a writer's employment deal. It does not hurt to ask, but I do not recall having seen one in recent years. In any event, it would probably not be more than $25,000. The studio figures that your guarantee covers this possibility.

Be aware of the terminology in your contract. Sometimes the initial draft of a writer's agreement will say that if you get sole *"written by"* credit, you will receive the bonus. As you will see in the chapter on writing credits, if you are the sole writer, you will probably get this credit. But if your material is based on someone else's story, then the story writer will probably receive a "story by" credit. In that case, you are the only *screenplay* writer to receive credit as distinguished from the story, and you will receive "screenplay by" credit. To cover this possibility, I ask that the language be changed to reflect that if you receive sole "written by" credit *or* sole "screenplay by" credit, you will receive the sole "screenplay by" bonus. The studio usually does intend to give the sole "screenplay by" bonus if you are the sole screenplay writer, even if someone else received "story by" credit, so the language should reflect it. Finally, if you think that your work might be used as the basis of a television movie or other television production, you should also add "teleplay by" credit to the list. The wording should thus be "If the writer receives sole 'written by,' 'screenplay by' or 'teleplay by' credit, the writer will receive the sole 'screenplay by' bonus." The same language would be used to describe the shared "screenplay by" bonuses. If the writer receives shared "written by," "screenplay by" or "teleplay by" credit, the writer will receive the shared "screenplay by" bonus.

The bonus is usually payable when credits are determined. If you are a member of the WGA or your employer is a signatory to the WGA, credit will be determined by arbitration if there is a dispute (see discussion below). Even if you are not a member of the WGA, credits are usually determined through arbitration. Most non-WGA companies will agree to use the same procedures and criteria prescribed by the Guild to determine credits, even if they are not signatories to the WGA.

If you are the sole writer on a movie, you may also ask to be paid your bonus earlier than the credit determination. Why should you wait until credits are determined (which will not be until after principal photography of the movie) to get your payment? Most studios agree that if no subsequent writer is hired prior to commencement of principal photography, you will receive your *shared* "screenplay by" bonus on commencement of principal photography of the picture. They will not give you the sole "screenplay by" bonus because the director or producer could rewrite the whole script while he is shooting it (not an uncommon occurrence) and directors and producers are entitled to claim writing credit. Note that for a director or producer to receive any credit, he or she must have contributed at least 50% of the screenplay. This requirement is designed to protect writers from losing their credits to persons who do not make their living solely by writing. It is an explicit recognition that credits are *very* important to writers.

Keep in mind that this provision is usually worded in such a way that any monies you receive before credit arbitration (i.e., on commencement of principal photography) are considered an *advance* against your bonus. In other words, if for some reason you do not get shared credit, you will have to repay the money. It is an unlikely scenario, but the studios protect themselves just the same.

3. Profits Based on Credit

The employed writer's entitlement to net profit participation is also based on credit. The norm is that the writer will receive 2 $1/2$% of 100% of the net profits for shared "screenplay by" credit, and 5% of 100% of the net profits for sole "screenplay by" credit. (See discussion above in Chapter Three I regarding the importance of adding the language *"of 100%"* in your contract.)

As discussed in the previous section, you want to be careful with the language that is used to define your entitlement. Be sure to use the words *written by*, *screenplay by* and *teleplay by* to describe your credit. In short, you do not want to lose your benefits because of the terminology. The studio intends to reward you if there are no other screen-writers or you share a screenplay credit, so make sure to cover yourself by referring to the various credit possibilities. Remember, someone else's entitlement to a "story by" credit should not cheat you of your *bonus* or *points*. It is one of the few norms that are decidedly in favor of the writer.

4. Passive Payments; Right to Write a Sequel or Other Subsequent Production

The requirements for passive payments are usually the same for writing assignments as they are for spec scripts. At the studios, the writer must receive sole separated rights (and sometimes shared) to receive payments. The same criterion is used for the writer's right to write a sequel or other subsequent production as with spec screen-plays. (Refer to the discussion in Chapter Three to refresh your understanding of these provisions.) The key to remember with writing assignments is that unless you write the first draft, you may never receive separated rights or, for that matter, credit. Thus, if you are asked to do a re-write of someone else's script, you should focus on the writing compensation. That is not to say that you should not negotiate other provisions for passive payments or the right to write a sequel. You never know, your script may be the script that is shot. There is an expression in Hollywood that refers to an extensive rewrite. It is called a "page one rewrite." It is not uncommon for a writer who is hired to do a rewrite to write a whole new script. It is not what the studio is paying for, but it happens. Thus, always protect yourself and if you are asked to write a rewrite and you contemplate major changes, negotiate the same points that you would have, had you been asked to write the first draft screenplay.

C. REWRITES, POLISHES AND OTHER WRITING SERVICES

When you are hired to write revisions on a screenplay that has already been written, your deal will look similar to an agreement for your writing services to write a first draft screenplay. The basic difference is the compensation. The initial compensation paragraph of the agreement will usually set forth your compensation for guaranteed services. This would be your "fixed compensation." There may be options for additional services.

Similar to an agreement for a writer who has been commissioned from the start, your agent will probably negotiate a sole screenplay bonus and a shared screenplay bonus. Obviously, when you are rewriting, the shared screenplay bonus is more important. You will also negotiate for passive payments. While it will be difficult for you to be accorded sole separated rights for purposes of being accorded passive payments, you should still negotiate this point. As noted above, many writers who are hired to do a rewrite end up doing a "page one rewrite," with new characters and so on. Under such circumstances, you might very well be entitled to at least shared separated rights and, depending on the studio, some compensation in this area.

In addition, you should set forth your contingent

compensation. Again, this will probably be based on sole and shared screenplay credit. All other provisions would basically be the same as contained in an agreement for a first draft screenplay.

A point to note: With enormous leverage, in some circumstances I have seen writers negotiate that they will receive their sole screenplay bonus if they get shared credit with anyone *other* than, for instance, the first writer (if the studio intends to throw out most of that writer's material). Or, sometimes you can get a bonus if the picture is made *without regard to credit.* Again, it is rare with studio deals, but under certain circumstances, particularly if you are paid very low money for rewriting services, you might insist upon some payment if the project gets made.

D. CERTIFICATE OF AUTHORSHIP

Writers are usually asked to sign a Certificate of Authorship in addition to a writing agreement. Like the short-form option and assignment (see Chapter Three G above), the main purpose of the Certificate is to register in the copyright office the fact that the employer of record owns the material which has been commissioned.

The Certificate of Authorship usually contains the writer's representations and warranties. It does not recite the salary.

The significance of the Certificate is that once signed, the employer owns the material. It is like the pink slip for a car. Ownership is absolute. For that reason, I like to have the Certificate make reference to the actual writer's agreement. Some studios will do this. Some will not. If there is any ambiguity in the contract or breach by the studio, the studio does not want the contract to affect its ownership of the material.

You should know that because of the legal significance of this piece of paper, studios will often agree to pay a writer his commencement monies upon the writer's signing of the Certificate, notwithstanding the fact that the long-form contract has not even been drafted yet. I do not recommend doing this, no matter how desperate for money you are. I like, at least, to see the long-form contract to make sure that all the financial provisions are accurately described. I also want to make sure there are no major problems with the contract. Remember, once you have signed the Certificate, you have no more leverage! You have signed away your rights. Once the major points are worked out in the long form, then it is up to you if you want to wait until every last *t* is crossed and *i* dotted. Some writers do. Some writers trust that the non-monetary provisions will get worked out in accordance with custom and practice, and they are usually right. Of course, it depends on who the employer is. If it is not a mainstream company, you are probably better off waiting until the whole contract is finalized.

Here is a sample Certificate of Authorship:

CERTIFICATE OF AUTHORSHIP

The undersigned hereby certifies that, pursuant to an agreement between _____ ("Producer") and _____ ("Writer"), for good and valuable consideration, the receipt and sufficiency of which is hereby acknowledged, the undersigned has rendered and will continue with the terms of said agreement to render services to Producer in connection with a proposed feature-length mo-

tion picture currently entitled "_____"
(the "Picture"); that all of the results and process of such
services are and will be created within the scope of Writer's
employment by Producer and are and will be deemed to
have been specially ordered or commissioned by Producer
to use as part of a motion picture, that such results and proceeds are and will be a work made for hire within the meaning of the United States Copyright Law and that Producer
shall be deemed to be the author thereof and the owner of
all rights therein, with the right to make such changes
therein and such use thereof as Producer may from time to
time determine as the author thereof. Writer hereby represents and warrants that, except with respect to material supplied to Writer by Producer, the results and proceeds of
Writer's services hereunder are and will be original with
Writer, do not and will not defame, infringe or violate the
rights or privacy or other rights of any third party and are not
the subject of any litigation or claim that might give rise to
litigation. Writer hereby agrees to indemnify Producer, its
licensees and assigns against any loss, cost or damage (including reasonable attorneys' fees) arising out of or in connection with any breach of any of the aforesaid representations, warranties or certifications, and to execute such
documents and do such other acts and deeds as may be
required by Producer or its licensees and assigns to further
evidence or effectuate Producer's rights hereunder. Producer
shall similarly indemnify Writer against any loss, cost or
damage (including reasonable attorneys' fees) arising out of
or in connection with any breach of any of Producer's representations to Writer. Producer's rights in and to the results
and proceeds of Writer's services hereunder may be freely
assigned and licensed and such assignment and/or license
shall be binding upon the undersigned and inure to the benefit of such assignee and/or licensee.

IN WITNESS WHEREOF, this document has been executed this _____ day of _____, 199_____.

_____
("Writer")

E. TELEVISION WRITERS SPECIFICALLY

1. The Television Marketplace as Distinguished from the Feature Marketplace

Before I discuss the primary differences between feature and TV writer deals, you must first understand the basic economic difference between feature development and television development. Apart from the differences in salaries, which can be staggering (well-known feature writers are usually paid in the hundreds of thousands of dollars as their up-front fee; movie-of-the-week writers make $75,000–100,000 tops as their up-front fee), the structure for financing features versus television productions is dramatically different. For features, studios are the major source of all financing. They usually own the material, finance production and distribute the product. In television, because of the Financial Interest and Syndication Rules, commonly called "the Fin-Syn Rules," the networks for the most part were prohibited from owning their own shows, and yet covered much of the financing. The FCC instituted these rules in the early days of television, due to the monopolistic control of all broadcasting by three powerful networks, the theory being that with power in the hands of so few, there was little opportunity to negotiate. Before the rules were implemented, networks tended to negotiate with a take-it-or-leave-it attitude. Thus, the producer of a proposed program would often be told by the network that the network would take all the profits in the show or the network would not put it on the air. Under the FCC rules, networks were thus prohibited from owning their own programs, with limited exceptions.

As a result of these rules, powerful producers became powerful suppliers of television programming, owning *all* rights in their shows. The networks became licensees looking to advertising dollars for their profits (which are not shared with the producer), and the producers looked to sales of their shows in syndication (basically airing of their product on independent stations after the initial airings on the network), and to foreign sales for their profits. Since networks were not given all the profits, they said they would not put up all the money to produce a show. A logical argument. The practice thus evolved for the network to put up most of the money for developing the script (actual writing costs), and in some cases a very small development fee for the producer ($5,000–$10,000 maximum), and 70%–80% of the cost of the show. The balance (or deficit) is generally provided through advances from foreign sales or syndication sales. For TV movies, a network usually gets two free runs for its investment. The network reserves the right to order additional runs for an additional fee, which would bring profit to the producer. Until recently, when the demand for American movies-of-the-week decreased abroad, a supplier producer knew before shooting the picture that it would be substantially in profit —sometimes as much as $1,000,000—based on foreign and syndication sales. This windfall was not uncommon for TV supplier producers (they are called ''supplier producers'' because they own the show and supply it to the network, as distinguished from hired producers, who are hired to actually produce the program).

The cost of producing shows has dramatically increased. The network license fees have not. (Generally the network pays $2,500,000 for a two-hour movie. The cost to produce a TV movie today is in excess of $3,000,000 generally.) Foreign sales are down and syndication sales are not as valuable, now that there are so many channels to watch and so much product in the marketplace. Producers are content to cover their deficit, earn handsome producing fees and, in success, to earn a profit. Gone are the guarantees. Today such shows are produced with only the *possibility* that they might earn out their advances from foreign territories or syndication (the advances cover the deficit), and the additional revenues required to turn a profit. Keep in mind that this might now take many years.

For a series, it might take many, *many* years. And keep in mind that throughout that time, the series is usually running at a deficit (meaning the cost is in excess of income—advances in series television do not usually cover the entire deficit). If and when the series as a whole (all episodes produced) is sold to syndication, there may be a profit. This sale usually occurs after the network run. At the high end, *The Bill Cosby Show* was sold for close to $1.25 million per episode to syndication. Many series, on the other hand, never see profit.

In short, producers are finding it much more difficult today to turn a profit in the traditional manner. Naturally, this has affected writers' salaries. Gone are the days when top television series writers were given million-dollar annual guarantees. Salaries have come down, and for those writers whose salaries were not very high to begin with, salaries have not gone up. It takes a major negotiation today to bring up movie-of-the-week writers by even $2,500!

You should be aware that the FCC recently voted to allow the networks to own more of their own programming, basically repeating the Financial Interest and Syndication rules. The FCC rationale: There is a lot of competition out there now and the networks are not as powerful as they used to be. Hollywood supplier producers (today the studios themselves are the supplier producers—they are the only ones who can afford to cover deficits, particularly for series) are outraged but, at this point, it seems unlikely that the FCC decision will be changed.

While I agree that there is more competition, I think it is also important to look at the nature of that competition. If you are a television series producer, for instance, with a mainstream, star-driven sitcom, will the competition finance a series of this type? Fox Television might, but the local cable station cannot. In other words, the competitors are not necessarily in the market for your product. So, again, you are down to the "big three" and Fox. The new Warner Bros. and Paramount networks may change things, we shall see.

2. Differences in Television Writing Deals

There are certain provisions, unique to a television writer's agreement, which you should be aware of.

Imagine that you have been asked to write a movie-of-the-week for television, for instance. If you are the first writer on the project, generally you will be employed to write more revisions than with a feature deal and for substantially less money. The typical television movie-of-the-week writer is usually engaged to write a story, a first draft teleplay, two sets of revisions and a polish. The writing periods are much shorter for a TV writer. TV executives work at a much faster pace. The Guild rules do not prescribe limitations regarding writing periods for television programs, and leave it to the writer and producer to work out their own schedule. Generally, writers do not take longer than eight weeks to deliver a first draft teleplay.

As indicated above, the salaries for writing television movies are substantially less than salaries customarily accorded for features. The range runs from $45,000 for all steps mentioned above to $72,000. The *top* end tends to be in the $75,000–$100,000 or more range unless you have incredible leverage. In television, the writer is usually given payment for the applicable writing step on *delivery*. (Sometimes, if you have leverage, you can get one half up front.) The reason: Networks only pay on delivery. Since most television writers are employed by supplier producers and since supplier producers look to the network for payment of the writer's fees, the supplier producer does not want to advance monies any sooner than the network pays. That is not to say that they do not make exceptions. And if they want you badly enough, they just might have to. As a rule, do not expect payment until delivery.

Television writers usually get a bonus based on credit, just like with features. In television, these are called "production bonuses." The range is generally $10,000 to $15,000 for sole "teleplay by" credit and $5,000 to $7,500 for shared "teleplay by" credit. Payment is made upon determination of credits, but the same principle applies regarding payment of the shared bonus on commencement of principal photography if no other writers are hired. (See discussion above in subchapter B.2.)

Finally, television writers tend to protect themselves

in case their teleplay is produced as a feature. Remember, for features, salaries are much higher. You should be entitled to more money if the teleplay is made as a feature, and you will be if you ask for it.

A common provision is the so-called "100/50/50" formula, usually referred to as a "theatrical release bonus." If the picture is exhibited as a feature in the United States (sometimes Canada is included) before it is shown on television, you will be entitled to another payment equal to 100% of the monies you were paid to write the TV script. (This should include the bonus, a point that must be established early in the negotiations.) As an example, if you received $80,000, including a bonus, for writing a television script, and the picture is released theatrically before airing on television in the United States, you will receive another $80,000 upon theatrical release of the picture. If the theatrical exhibition is after the television run, then you will receive a payment equal to 50% of your original monies on release of the picture theatrically in the United States, and another payment equal to 50% of your original monies on showing of the picture theatrically outside the United States. In no event will your aggregate bonus exceed 100% of your original monies. Using the example above, if the picture is only released theatrically outside the United States (this may happen, for instance, with a Showtime or HBO movie) after its initial run, then you will receive another $40,000. (Note that if you are an established feature writer, you may sometimes be able to negotiate that you will get your full feature film compensation if the picture is released theatrically although this provision is rare.)

3. Writing a Series: Compensation

If you are hired to write a pilot script for a series, the main points that you want to negotiate are (1) your up-front compensation, (2) a royalty for each episode produced if a series is ordered based on your script, (3) a bonus for a production order for the series and (4) profit participation. Bonuses and profit participations are usually based on credit. For a television series, it is the writer who is awarded the "created by" credit who gets the bonus. (In television, the *creator* of a series is accorded "created by" credit, meaning that the characters and plot in the pilot episode are substantially the same as those created by the writer—the pilot episode being the prototype episode for the series.) The criterion used to determine "created by" credit is similar to that used to determine separated rights for features. (See discussion in Chapter Three L above.) As with features, several different writers may be brought on board. It is not uncommon to see shared "created by" credit. There is usually one royalty amount negotiated for sole "created by" credit and a lesser amount for shared "created by" credit. Top writers may receive as much as $5,000 or more per episode for sole "created by" credit, reducible down to 50% of that amount per episode for shared "created by" credit. A fine point of negotiation in respect of the series royalty, just as with passive payments based on separated rights, is to ask that the royalty be reducible by amounts *actually* paid to another writer who receives shared "created by" credit to a floor of 50% of the sole "created by" credit. That way, if another writer is receiving a much lower royalty, your royalty will not automatically be reduced to your floor. Example: You receive a $4,000 royalty per episode for sole "created by" credit, reducible to $2,000 per episode for shared "created by" credit, by royalties paid to another writer entitled to receive shared "created by" credit. You receive shared "created by" credit with another writer. The other writer is entitled to only $1,000 per episode as his/her royalty. In this example, you would receive $3,000 per episode. Successful writers are sometimes able to negotiate a royalty regardless of credit. This royalty is usually slightly less than the shared "created by" royalty. If the shared royalty is $2,000 per episode, the royalty regardless of credit would probably be $1,500 per episode.

Often a production bonus will be paid if a series is ordered by the network. This is also based on "created by" credit with two amounts negotiated. One for sole "created by" credit—at the top end, $15,000—and one for shared "created by" credit—usually one half the sole "created by" bonus amount. The payments may be further reduced depending on the number of episodes initially ordered. For instance, the bonuses may be conditioned on twelve episodes being ordered. If fewer are ordered, the bonus would be prorated, usually down to a floor of six episodes. Using the example above, if eight episodes were ordered and you receive sole "created by" credit, you would be entitled to $8/12 \times \$15,000$ or $10,000. Just as with the royalty, successful writers are sometimes able to negotiate a production bonus regardless of credit. Again, it will be somewhat less than the shared credit production bonus.

The other main area of negotiation with a television series is your profit participation. Successful writers in television usually receive a piece of adjusted gross, although with a first-run syndication series, net profits are more customary. The reason: Net profits are even more meaningless in television than they are for features. (Review the discussion regarding net profits participation in Chapter Three I.2 above.) The main reason is cash flow. The major portion of the revenues earned on a hit movie are earned early in the picture's release. Theatrical exhibition and home video exhibition generally account for 42%–45% of a picture's revenues. Thus, it is possible to recover all expenditures on a feature if there is an enormous infusion of cash at the outset, thereby cutting down on the interest charges on the unrecouped production and distribution expenses that continue to accrue until the picture reaches breakeven. In television, by contrast, the major portion of the profit-making revenues are earned way after the series is launched—when the series is sold to syndication (i.e., sales to off-network programming, usually after the initial network run). In the meantime, the series has been accumulating substantial deficits and interest is being charged on that deficit *over* many years. The potential for profit is thus much less with a series, unless the syndication revenues are substantial. And if the series syndication sale does not produce big numbers, it may not be profitable. The reason: The deficits are too large and the syndication sales disappointing. Studios may brave a deficit, even a huge one, with the hope that syndication sales will be substantial. Sometimes they miscalculate. Sometimes, even though a series may be on the air for many years, it does not generate net profits or even adjusted gross, for that matter. In recent years, hour-long series have not fared well at all in syndication sales, and half-hour series have to be extremely successful (e.g., *Cheers)* to generate sufficient revenues for profits to be made.

Recall that the key difference between net profits and adjusted gross is the distribution fee charged. In television, with an adjusted gross definition, the supplier company eliminates its distribution fee altogether on the network sale and may only charge the actual distribution fee that it is charged by an outside syndication sales company, if any, or a very low fee if it is itself the syndicator (which is often the case nowadays with series).

If you are only able to negotiate a net profits participation, you will probably be entitled to 5% of 100% of the net profits for your sole "created by" credit, and 2 $1/2$% of 100% of the net profits for shared "created by" credit. (This may be higher in television.) If you are lucky to get adjusted gross, it will usually be 2 $1/2$% of 100% of the adjusted gross for sole "created by" credit, reducible to 1 $1/4$% of the adjusted gross for shared "created by" credit. (Again, it may be higher in television.) One common formula for adjusted gross participants is to grant the writer the higher of 5% of 100% of the net profit or 2 $1/2$% of 100% of the adjusted gross for sole "created by" credit, and the higher of 2 $1/2$% of 100% of the net profits and 1 $1/4$% of 100% of the adjusted gross for shared "created by" credit. That way, the writer is protected if the net profits formula is higher.

One way to protect against the possibility that there will be no net profits (or even adjusted gross, for that matter) is to negotiate a guaranteed advance against your participation (your entitlement to a share of net profits or adjusted gross is also referred to as your "participation"), if the series lasts. The first advance would be paid after the sixty-sixth episode. It is generally thought that at least sixty-seven original episodes of a series must be ordered by the network (in short, going into the fourth year) in order for a syndication sale to mean anything. Further advances are often awarded at eighty-nine episodes (going into a fifth year) and at one hundred eleven episodes (going into a sixth year). The advance provision might look something like this:

If Company produces at least 67 episodes of the series, provided the writer is entitled to receive his profit participation, Company agrees to advance writer against writer's share of the series' net profits, if any, and solely out of positive cash flow *[in other words, by then the license fee from the network and other revenues are greater than the cost of producing the episode—including payment of Company's 10% overhead fee (the norm for overhead is 10%, but it is sometimes as high as 15% and this fee is negotiable if you have a lot of leverage)]*, the following sums:

(a) In connection with the first 67 episodes produced (66 episodes is usually after 3 years so 67 episodes would be going into the fourth year) Company agrees to advance writer the sum of One Thousand Dollars ($1,000) per episode.

(b) Said advance shall increase retroactively to One Thousand Seven Hundred Fifty Dollars ($1,750) per episode if Company produces at least 89 (88 episodes is usually after 4 years so 89 episodes is going into the fifth year) episodes of said series.

(c) Said advance shall increase retroactively to Three Thousand Five Hundred Dollars ($3,500) per episode if Company produces at least 111 episodes of said series.

The advances are usually payable immediately after the 67th, 89th and 111th episode respectively.

If you are hired to write the pilot script, you should decide whether you want to continue as a writer with the show beyond the pilot script. Writers of episodes (generally referred to as staff writers) receive WGA minimum compensation to write episodes. For a story and teleplay, the minimum is $15,172 for a one-half-hour network show and $22,315 for a one-hour network show in 1994 (5/1/94–5/1/95). If you want to continue writing the series, then you should ask to write a minimum number of episodes per broadcast order.

4. Writing a Series: Yearly Guarantee

Most writers who write pilot scripts become story editors and producers of the series. The pay is substantially higher. If you are in that position, you will probably not want to write more than a handful of individual episodes. (See Section 5 below.)

Writers who did not write the pilot episode are often employed as staff writers. If you are in this category, again you will want to negotiate a guaranteed number of episodes and the opportunity, at some point, to render additional services, as story editor, co-producer and even producer if you stay with the show long enough.

5. Producing or Executive Producing a Series

Aside from the stars, the hotshots in the television series arena are the writers who also produce or executive produce the series—oversee the staff writers and the production of the show. These dual-capacity persons are generally referred to as "hyphenates." At the lowest level, a hyphenate may be a story editor on the series. If you have created a series (and received sole "created by" credit), odds are you will be able to negotiate to be at least a story editor or a consultant on the show. The next level is co-producer and then producer and/or executive producer. What this means, aside from a lot more work, is that you will earn a lot more money *and* be entitled to a greater share of the profits. You will also have a guarantee that you will be intricately involved with the production of your series. This tradition probably had its roots in the early days of television when entrepreneurial individuals could achieve great success, and often wore many hats.

A successful producer or executive producer may receive as much as $30,000 *per* episode to produce a series. These amounts are generally bumped about 5% for each subsequent year, and the bumps are cumulative. Thus, $31,500 in the second year, $33,025 in the third year, and so on. Co-producer salaries today are usually $7,500 to $15,000 per episode. As you can see, it adds up. Consultants may be paid $5,000 to $7,500 per episode. Generally, your position is elevated over time. You may be a consultant or story editor in the first year, a co-producer in the second year and a producer in the third year. Of course, if you have produced or executive produced a series before, you will probably start out as a producer or executive producer.

Unless you have enormous leverage, most companies will not guarantee that you will be locked as a producer, executive producer or co-producer to a series for the life of the show. If the ratings are sluggish, supplier companies want the ability to bring in fresh blood. Producers, executive producers, co-producers and even story editors are usually attached for two years, after which time they are guaranteed employment as consultants on the show for several more years, and sometimes for the life of the show, at a reduced salary. Generally, this salary is 50% of the salary that was paid before the switch to consultant. This amount is usually *not* subject to increases. As an example, if, in the second year of a series, you receive a producing/ executive producing fee of $30,000 or more per episode, you will then receive a salary as a consultant of $15,000 per episode for a period of time, maybe even for the life of the show. Of course, if the show is enormously successful, the studio will probably beg you to stay on as a producer, and at that point you may be able to negotiate the top rate in town.

Producers and executive producers also receive profits. Indeed, one's profit participation as a writer might double or triple as a result of being a producer or executive producer. As a writer entitled to sole "created by" credit, your share of the profits would probably be 5% of 100% of the net profits against 2 ½% of 100% of the adjusted gross. It is not uncommon for a top writer/producer to negotiate to receive 10% of 100% of the net profits against 5% of 100% of the adjusted gross.

The producer's/executive producer's profit participation may also be increased for additional years of service as producer/executive producer on the show. In other words, the company may increase your share if you stay with the show longer. This point requires a lot of leverage to get. I just want to make you aware of the possibilities. The producer/executive producer would also be entitled to a theatrical release bonus (100/50/50) (see subchapter 2 above) on his/her salary as a producer/executive producer, if the pilot, for instance, is released as a feature. This would be a rare occurrence, but you should provide for it just the same.

In short, if you create a series, you will want some guarantee that you will be involved in the production of the series if it goes. Obviously, you have to learn how to produce it, so start at a lower level as a story editor, consultant or co-producer, with increased responsibilities in subsequent years of the series. Be sure to get yourself in there somehow. At some point, you will have gained enough experience to be guaranteed the right to produce a show that you create, and with it, the creative and financial rewards.

CHAPTER FIVE

COPYRIGHT, IDEAS, TITLES

A. DEFINITION AND BENEFITS

U.S. copyright law derives from our Constitution.

> The Congress shall have power . . . to promote the prog-
> ress of science and useful arts, by securing for limited times
> to authors and inventors the exclusive right to their respec-
> tive writings and discoveries. (U.S. Constitution, Article I,
> Section 8.)

If your work is an original creation, then it is automatically protected under copyright law. "Copyright protection subsists . . . in original works of authorship fixed in
the tangible medium of expression, now known or later
developed, from which they can be perceived, reproduced
or otherwise communicated, either directly or with the aid
of a machine or device." Works of authorship include literary works, musical works, dramatic works, pantomimes and
choreographic works, pictorial graphic and sculptural

works, motion picture and sound recordings. A writing is a work of authorship in a fixed form.

Copyright is a property right. Think of it in a way like the house or car that you own—it can be transferred, passed on by will, mortgaged and so on. Copyright is established by the single act of original creation and embodiment of that creation in a fixed, tangible form as listed above. Under the old Copyright Act (1909), certain formalities were required to obtain copyright protection in the first place. For instance, under the 1909 act, registration was a prerequisite for copyright protection and had to be made within twenty-eight years of publication. Under the new act (1976), effective January 1, 1978, no formalities are required and you own a copyright in your work *when* you write it; nothing more.

What if your work is based on other material, such as a true story or a book? You still own the copyright in your work. In such instance, you do not own the copyright in the underlying material—the material that existed before you put pen to paper and created your *own* work—but you do own copyright in your additions and creations.

The major exception to the rule that the writer or original creator owns the copyright in his/her material is the "work for hire." As discussed in Chapter One, when you are hired to write, your material is owned by the employer and the employer holds the copyright. Remember, the employer is called the author!

The duration of copyright protection depends on the nature of the work and when it was created. If it was created after January 1, 1978, the term of copyright lasts from the time of creation until fifty years after the author's death. In the case of a work for hire, the duration of copyright protection is seventy-five years from the year of first "publication" or one hundred years from the year of creation, whichever occurs first. *Publication,* in this context, means that the work is first distributed to the public, not necessarily that it is published by a book company.

Aside from establishing ownership in a literary work, copyright provides the owner with the right to sue in the case of any unauthorized use of the copyright owner's material. Just as a homeowner can sue for property damage in an action for trespass or encroachment, the copyright owner can bring an action for infringement when his/her rights are violated. "Anyone who violates any of the exclusive rights of the copyright owner . . . is an infringer of the copyright." (17 U.S.C.§ 501 [a] [1976].) Examples of infringement are unauthorized copying and adaptation of someone else's work. The key element of any such suit is to prove that the infringer actually copied the work by establishing similarity and that the infringer had access to the similar work.

The defense to any infringement suit, on the other hand, is to prove that one did not copy someone else's work. As long as you can prove your independent creation of your material, you are not an infringer.

One way to establish proof of creation is to register your work with the U.S. Copyright Office. The work can be registered at any time during the copyright term. Remember, registration is not necessary for copyright protection, but it helps to prove when the work was created. If someone claims that you infringed, and you are able to prove that you created your work before the person claiming infringement, that person has no case. And if someone copies your work and you can prove that you created your work before the infringer, such proof will be helpful. In fact, registration is essential in order to bring a suit for copyright infringement, although registration may be made after the act of infringement has occurred. If you wait until after the infringement occurs, however, you will not be able to recover certain damages and attorneys' fees.

Obviously, the earlier you register your work, the earlier you will establish its creation. Many writers register their material when it is completed. If you plan to take a long time in finishing your work, then you may want to register major portions as you go along. This can be time consuming and you have to pay each time that you do it (as you will note below, it is not that costly), but if you are concerned about protecting your rights and that someone might rip you off, you should do it. (You can also accomplish the same goal by registering your work with the Writers Guild.) The Guild maintains a script registration service for members and non-members. This is valuable as a way to establish proof of creation and time of creation. Simply submit your screenplay to the Writers Guild of America Registration Office. There is one in Los Angeles, and one in New York. The cost is $10.00 per submission. Non-members can take advantage of the system for $20.00 per submission. The Guild will place a copy of your screenplay in their files and give you a record of the time of registration. For more information, contact the Writers Guild of America, West (Telephone: [310] 550-1000), or the Writers Guild of America, East (Telephone: [212] 767-7800).

The copyright registration process (the better route) is fairly simple. Write to the Copyright Office, Library of Congress, Washington, D.C. 20559 and request Form PA. Complete the form and submit a copy of the screenplay or material that you want to protect. The cost is $20.00. The normal process can take in excess of three months, so be patient. But know that the date of *submission* is determinative. You should also know that your work will be examined. Thus, you cannot claim copyright registration in something that the Copyright Office knows has been copied.

Notice is not required to obtain copyright, but it is helpful and puts the world on notice that you own the copyright. Notice consists of three elements: (1) the word *copyright* or ©; (2) your name; and (3) the year of first publication (when the work is offered to the public). Usually, notice is placed on the title page, but that is not a requirement. It must be "affixed" to the copies in such a manner and location as to give reasonable notice of the claim of copyright. For instance, "© Stephen F. Breimer 1995."

Here is a sample Form PA:

FORM PA
UNITED STATES COPYRIGHT OFFICE

REGISTRATION NUMBER

PA   PAU

EFFECTIVE DATE OF REGISTRATION

Month   Day   Year

DO NOT WRITE ABOVE THIS LINE. IF YOU NEED MORE SPACE, USE A SEPARATE CONTINUATION SHEET.

1 TITLE OF THIS WORK ▼

PREVIOUS OR ALTERNATIVE TITLES ▼

NATURE OF THIS WORK ▼ See instructions

2

a   NAME OF AUTHOR ▼

DATES OF BIRTH AND DEATH
Year Born ▼   Year Died ▼

Was this contribution to the work a "work made for hire"?
☐ Yes
☐ No

AUTHOR'S NATIONALITY OR DOMICILE
Name of Country
OR { Citizen of ▶
{ Domiciled in ▶

WAS THIS AUTHOR'S CONTRIBUTION TO THE WORK
Anonymous? ☐ Yes ☐ No
Pseudonymous? ☐ Yes ☐ No
If the answer to either of these questions is "Yes," see detailed instructions.

NATURE OF AUTHORSHIP Briefly describe nature of the material created by this author in which copyright is claimed. ▼

NOTE

Under the law, the "author" of a "work made for hire" is generally the employer, not the employee (see instructions). For any part of this work that was "made for hire" check "Yes" in the space provided, give the employer (or other person for whom the work was prepared) as "Author" of that part, and leave the space for dates of birth and death blank.

b   NAME OF AUTHOR ▼

DATES OF BIRTH AND DEATH
Year Born ▼   Year Died ▼

Was this contribution to the work a "work made for hire"?
☐ Yes
☐ No

AUTHOR'S NATIONALITY OR DOMICILE
Name of Country
OR { Citizen of ▶
{ Domiciled in ▶

WAS THIS AUTHOR'S CONTRIBUTION TO THE WORK
Anonymous? ☐ Yes ☐ No
Pseudonymous? ☐ Yes ☐ No
If the answer to either of these questions is "Yes," see detailed instructions.

NATURE OF AUTHORSHIP Briefly describe nature of the material created by this author in which copyright is claimed. ▼

c   NAME OF AUTHOR ▼

DATES OF BIRTH AND DEATH
Year Born ▼   Year Died ▼

Was this contribution to the work a "work made for hire"?
☐ Yes
☐ No

AUTHOR'S NATIONALITY OR DOMICILE
Name of Country
OR { Citizen of ▶
{ Domiciled in ▶

WAS THIS AUTHOR'S CONTRIBUTION TO THE WORK
Anonymous? ☐ Yes ☐ No
Pseudonymous? ☐ Yes ☐ No
If the answer to either of these questions is "Yes," see detailed instructions.

NATURE OF AUTHORSHIP Briefly describe nature of the material created by this author in which copyright is claimed. ▼

3 YEAR IN WHICH CREATION OF THIS WORK WAS COMPLETED This information must be given in all cases. ◀ Year

DATE AND NATION OF FIRST PUBLICATION OF THIS PARTICULAR WORK
Complete this information Month ▶ _____ Day ▶ _____ Year ▶ _____ ◀ Nation
ONLY if this work has been published.

4 COPYRIGHT CLAIMANT(S) Name and address must be given even if the claimant is the same as the author given in space 2. ▼

See instructions before completing this space.

TRANSFER If the claimant(s) named here in space 4 are different from the author(s) named in space 2, give a brief statement of how the claimant(s) obtained ownership of the copyright. ▼

APPLICATION RECEIVED

ONE DEPOSIT RECEIVED

TWO DEPOSITS RECEIVED

REMITTANCE NUMBER AND DATE

DO NOT WRITE HERE OFFICE USE ONLY

MORE ON BACK ▶ • Complete all applicable spaces (numbers 5-9) on the reverse side of this page.
• See detailed instructions. • Sign the form at line 8.

DO NOT WRITE HERE
Page 1 of _____ pages

DO NOT WRITE ABOVE THIS LINE. IF YOU NEED MORE SPACE, USE A SEPARATE CONTINUATION SHEET.

PREVIOUS REGISTRATION Has registration for this work, or for an earlier version of this work, already been made in the Copyright Office?
☐ Yes ☐ No If your answer is "Yes," why is another registration being sought? (Check appropriate box) ▼
☐ This is the first published edition of a work previously registered in unpublished form.
☐ This is the first application submitted by this author as copyright claimant.
☐ This is a changed version of the work, as shown by space 6 on this application.
If your answer is "Yes," give: **Previous Registration Number ▼**   **Year of Registration ▼**

5

DERIVATIVE WORK OR COMPILATION Complete both space 6a & 6b for a derivative work; complete only 6b for a compilation.
a. **Preexisting Material** Identify any preexisting work or works that this work is based on or incorporates. ▼

b. **Material Added to This Work** Give a brief, general statement of the material that has been added to this work and in which copyright is claimed. ▼

See instructions before completing this space.

6

DEPOSIT ACCOUNT If the registration fee is to be charged to a Deposit Account established in the Copyright Office, give name and number of Account.
Name ▼   **Account Number ▼**

7

CORRESPONDENCE Give name and address to which correspondence about this application should be sent. Name/Address/Apt/City/State/Zip ▼

                    Area Code & Telephone Number ▶

Be sure to give your daytime phone number

CERTIFICATION* I, the undersigned, hereby certify that I am the
Check only one ▼
☐ author
☐ other copyright claimant
☐ owner of exclusive right(s)
☐ authorized agent of _____
                    Name of author or other copyright claimant, or owner of exclusive right(s) ▲

of the work identified in this application and that the statements made
by me in this application are correct to the best of my knowledge.

Typed or printed name and date ▼ If this is a published work, this date must be the same as or later than the date of publication given in space 3.

                                                            date ▶ _____

☞ Handwritten signature (X) ▼

8

MAIL CERTIFI-CATE TO	Name ▼	Have you: • Completed all necessary spaces? • Signed your application in space 8? • Enclosed check or money order for $10 payable to Register of Copyrights? • Enclosed your deposit material with the application and fee? **MAIL TO:** Register of Copyrights, Library of Congress, Washington, D.C. 20559
Certificate will be mailed in window envelope	Number/Street/Apartment Number ▼	
	City/State/ZIP ▼	

9

B. TITLES

Titles are not protected by copyright. The basic rule is that the author has no inherent right in the title to his production, screenplay, play or book title. *(Jackson v. Universal International Pictures,* 36 Cal. 2d 116 [1950].) Only when the title has acquired a so-called "secondary meaning"—that is, when the title is established in the public mind—is the author entitled to its exclusive use. *Gone With the Wind,* for instance, is known as the title of a book and a motion picture. The public immediately thinks of a specific movie based on a specific book when the title is mentioned, and the association is clear.

How many persons need to have the required association? There is no set number and it does not have to be masses. The "public" need not necessarily consist of people throughout the nation, but it should be a substantial number of persons. If you submit your script to twenty producers, do not count on being able to keep the title. On the other end of the spectrum, it is clear that once a picture is made and distributed to the public, the title acquires secondary meaning.

Suppose your script is the hottest in town and everyone is buzzing about it. *The Last Boy Scout* was one such script and no one dared to steal the title. "Secondary meaning" had something to do with it. *Everyone* in Hollywood at the time knew about that script. It was written up in the trade papers *(The Hollywood Reporter* and *Variety).* Also, as a practical matter, regardless of secondary meaning, no one wants to be known as a rip-off artist. It would have been an obvious rip-off to have used that title at the time.

What if your title has already been used often in other

contexts? If the title is found to have numerous uses, such that the public does not associate it with one particular business, then you may be able to use it. For instance, take the title *Acme Loves You.* There are many businesses with the title Acme. Just look in the phone book. It is doubtful that any particular Acme business would sue, because the public as a whole does not associate the name *Acme* with one particular business. On the other hand, the word *Pepsi-Cola*™ is specific and trademarked. You should stay away from it.

While there are no black-and-white rules, the real key to using any title is whether its use will result in confusion in the public's mind as to the source of the work. It is not necessary that there be actual confusion by the public, and the mere possibility that a consumer may be misled is not enough. There must be a *likelihood* of confusion. Is the similar title used in the same market? Has the other title been used commercially in recent years? Is it a forgotten title? It might have achieved secondary meaning many years ago, but does that secondary meaning still exist? After a certain period of time, secondary meaning can disappear if the title is no longer associated with a particular work.

What if your title uses only some of the words from another title? There is a case that involves the comparison of the title *The Love Bug* (a Disney movie) and "The Love Bug Will Bite You (If You Don't Watch Out)" (a song). *(Tomlin v. Walt Disney Productions,* 18 Cal. App. 3d 226 [1971].) In that instance, even though the alleged owner of the song claimed that his song had been nicknamed "The Love Bug," he lost. One title was used for a song; the other for a film. No likelihood of confusion was found.

Some producers will widely publicize a film title prior

to production of a picture—with ads in the trades (short for *trade papers*), articles, posters at film festivals and film trade-markets and the like (such as Cannes and the American Film Market). Such evidence is usually compelling and usually stops another party from using the same title. A producer can thus help you to protect your title in this manner.

Producers also have another way to protect titles which is not available to the writer. The Motion Picture Association has a Title Registration Bureau. All of the studios and many major production companies and producers subscribe to it. The way it works, subscribers register the titles they want to use. If someone else has already registered a particular title, the second person to register is put on a waiting list. If the first party to register the title does not use the title (i.e., produce a picture) within a certain period of time (with extensions, eighteen months to two years), then that party loses the title, unless the second registerer on the list gives permission to the first to extend. The second party might give permission if he does not think the first party will produce a picture soon and the second party is not ready to make a picture (remember, once you are first on the list, the clock starts ticking). If you sell your screenplay to a studio or a producer that is a subscriber to the Motion Picture Association Title Registration Bureau, they will immediately register your title for you, so your title can also be protected that way.

One problem with the MPAA system is that only subscribers are bound by the terms. A non-subscriber is free to use a subscriber's title, unless the subscriber's title has achieved secondary meaning. Of course, if the non-subscriber sells the project to a subscriber, e.g., an independent producer independently finances a film and then sells it to a major studio, the major studio will have to play by the Title Registration Bureau rules. And if another subscriber to the Bureau has already registered the title at that time, then the studio will not be able to use it as long as that other subscriber has priority.

The other problem with the MPAA system, for writers in particular, is that protection is for the subscriber, not for you. That does not mean that the subscriber will be able to use your title if the subscriber's rights in your screenplay lapse. But once that subscriber's right to your material does lapse, so does your protection under this system. Of course, you are still protected by the secondary meaning doctrine, and if there is enough buzz about your title and enough people have seen it, odds are it will not be ripped off.

In short, there are many variables. Clearly, simple submission of your script to several producers, absent unusual circumstances such as *The Last Boy Scout* example, is not enough to establish secondary meaning. If you have a great title, you might want to save it until you sell your script to a producer or studio and it looks like it is going to be produced. That way, no one will know about it until something can be done to try to protect it.

C. IDEAS

Ideas are not protected by copyright law. The essence of copyright law is that the protection granted to a copyrighted work extends only to the particular expression of the idea and never to the idea itself *(Mazer v. Stein,* 347 U.S. 201, 217, 218 [1954]); *(Baker v. Selden* 101 U.S. 99 [1879]).

Nevertheless, under certain very limited circumstances, ideas may be protected by express or implied contract. One thing is for sure: if you "blurt out" your idea, such as at a cocktail party, there is no protection at all. So be careful what you disclose.

The main reason that ideas are not protected by copyright derives from the basic principle of copyright law that only independent original creations should be protected. On the other hand, an idea, a concept or a common plot is not protected because certain concepts and plots are universal and must be available to all authors. Boy meets girl as a plot, for instance: if one author were entitled to copyright this concept, no one else would be able to use it. For that reason, the material worthy of copyright protection must be sufficiently original in order to qualify.

The law also recognizes, however, that under certain circumstances, it is unfair for people to steal ideas, particularly in Hollywood where unique ideas are often the springboard for successful pictures. One famous case (*Blaustein v. Burton,* 9 Cal. App. 3d 161, 88 Cal. Rpts. 319 [1970]) involved a producer who came up with the idea of casting Richard Burton and Elizabeth Taylor in *The Taming of the Shrew.* The producer also came up with the idea of using Franco Zeffirelli as the director, eliminating the play-within-a-play device contained in Shakespeare's play, the idea of including in the film version two key scenes which in the play occurred offstage (i.e., the wedding scene and the wedding night scene) and the idea of filming in Italy. No question that these were the producer's ideas and they were unique. Copyright law does not cover such unique concepts.

However, the court held that a contract may be established if it is clear that the person disclosing the idea will be paid if his idea is used. (The producer in this case unfortunately had not established a contract.) To best protect yourself, the notion of compensation should be agreed upon *before* the idea is disclosed. Such agreement may be implied under the circumstances (called an "implied-in-fact contract": for instance, a professional producer who makes his living by producing films discloses the idea; it is clear that he intends to produce the film and receive a salary for so doing) or express (i.e., before you disclose an idea, have the listener actually agree that you will be paid if the listener uses it. The listener must also have an opportunity to reject the idea on the terms offered).

The law also recognizes a promise to pay immediately after the idea is disclosed *(Donahue v. Ziv Television Programs, Inc.,* 245 Cal. App. 2d 593, 54 Cal. Rpts. 130 [1966]), but once you have blurted out your idea, if the listener to your idea makes no such promise, you are out of luck. "The idea man who blurts out his idea without having first made his bargain has no one to blame but himself for the loss of his bargaining power." This case involved the similarity between the series *Sea Hunt* and a similar format for an underwater legion series which had previously been submitted to the producer of *Sea Hunt*. There was no other similarity between the two series, other than concept, which is why a suit for copyright infringement was out of the question. Indeed, this is the reason that one often sees movies with common themes, even in the same year. Studios often race to be the first to capitalize on a hot new concept (e.g., there are numerous detective movies, lover-turned-killer movies, and so on). As long as the commonality is concept, there is no danger, and even if there are similar plot points, as long as one party does not actually copy the other, there is also no copyright infringement.

Remember, to prove infringement, one has to prove that there was actual copying by access *and* similarity.

The *Sea Hunt* case also stated that the amount of the compensation does not have to be specifically agreed upon, although certainly it helps. A court can establish the value, particularly in the entertainment industry, by testimony indicating what writers have been paid under similar circumstances.

Applying the law in this area, ideally you would handle idea submissions in the following manner: You have a great idea. You want someone to pay you to write a script about it. You manage to set up a meeting with a producer. You should say to the producer, "I have a great idea. If you decide to use it, you must pay me a certain sum to write." If you have already been employed by someone and have a quote (a "quote" is your previous salary to write), you might say ". . . you must pay me to write at my going rate." If he says no, then do not disclose the idea. If he says yes and agrees to your terms, you have a deal. Your safest bet, of course, is to put it in writing. A simple letter agreement will do. Or write a letter and say, "Unless I hear back from you to the contrary, this confirms our deal." While self-serving, the burden is then on the producer to respond that he does not agree to the terms.

To say the least, this is not an easy process, particularly if you are a beginner. Most producers will probably respond by saying, "I'm not going to agree to anything until I hear your idea." If you do not have substantial credentials or even if you do, most producers will not be bothered with such formalities and they will pass on the opportunity. It is just too complicated and leaves them open to lawsuits. Alternatively, they may ask for you to sign a submission agreement. In essence, it requires you to waive any rights you may have if that producer produces a film with the same or similar idea to yours.

The better path for you to follow is to flesh out your idea at least to the treatment stage (a "treatment" is a detailed outline of the plot, description of characters, and so on). That way you have copyright protection and you never have to bother with the vagaries of establishing an implied-in-fact contract if an unscrupulous producer tries to rip you off. Remember, you will have to sue if you get ripped off, and that is quite costly. However, with a treatment (tangible evidence of your original creation) and a record of your submission, even the *threat* of a suit may make the producer think twice about using your material. In such instance, your tangible evidence creates a solid threat of copyright infringement if the producer tries to steal your material.

As a practical matter, established writers often pitch story ideas to studios and producers (usually complete with a plot summary and character description) and there is an understanding within the industry that the writer will be hired if the studio likes the pitch. To the extent that the pitch is more than idea, there is legal protection. There is also relationship protection. Most established writers are represented by established agents. Agents would not submit material or set up meetings if there was a substantial risk that their clients might be ripped off as a result of such pitch meetings. That is not to say that it never happens. In general, the Hollywood system recognizes certain rules in the course of doing business. Studios will usually not want to proceed to develop a project without using the writer if there is evidence of the meeting and the pitch is sufficiently detailed.

D. DROIT MORALE

All American contracts require the author to waive his right of *"droit morale." Droit morale* is a European concept, prevalent particularly in France and Italy. In those countries, by law, authors are granted rights, non-waiverable, which are personal to them. These laws limit the changes which the buyer of an author's work can make. The moral rights of authors ensure that the writer be named as the author and specifically prevent the buyer of a literary work from making changes which deform or mischaracterize the original intent of the author or reflect poorly on his professional reputation. They also prevent the buyer from falsely attributing written material to an author (for instance when a famous writer's work has been changed, yet the publisher or studio still wants to exploit the famous writer's name).

This concept is anathema to U.S. studios. As indicated above, their basic philosophy is they pay for it, they can do whatever they want with it. Therefore, you must agree not to assert any rights of *"droit morale."*

E. CHAIN OF TITLE

The film business is an extremely lucrative one. Where there is money to be made, there are bound to be lawsuits launched by persons seeking to get their share of the pie. Of course, many such suits are justified and when a writer's material is stolen, someone has to pay. In subchapter A above, I discussed the principles used in determining the outcome in legitimate copyright infringement suits. On the other hand, many such lawsuits are unmerited and are

launched by persons seeking to gain, essentially by muddy-
ing the waters.

Throughout this book, I have pointed to the specter
of nuisance suits and the reality that there are unscrupulous writers and producers about who seek to be rewarded
by claiming they have rights in a project. The main problem is that studios tend to shy away from projects if there is
any doubt about the ownership of a script. Studios want
what they call a clean "chain of title." Chain of title estab-
lishes that the seller of a screenplay does, in fact, own the
screenplay. For instance, if the screenplay is based on a
book, the owner of a screenplay should also have the rights
to a book or know that they are available.

The studio will examine the written documents that
establish ownership in the seller. They will also ask for full
disclosure of any claims known to the seller by any persons
claiming that they own the screenplay or that the screenplay infringes on such person's rights in any manner whatsoever.

Producers who claim they have rights in a project,
notwithstanding the writer's position, create what is called
a "cloud" on the chain of title or doubts about ownership.
If there is such a cloud, the studio will want it removed
quickly before they make a deal. Unfortunately, removal of
the "cloud" usually requires making a deal with the person clouding the chain of title. It is much quicker and
probably less costly than going to court—so the creator of
the cloud wins by trying to mess things up. A recent case,
however, indicates that courts may put a damper on such
attempts to muddy the waters. In an unpublished opinion,
Max Baer, Jr., v. American Broadcasting Co., B.O. 58056 Supe-
rior Court Case No. C601592, 2nd District, Court of Ap-
peal (1992), the court examined the following fact pat-

tern: ABC tried to obtain the rights to the song "Like a Virgin," which song was to be used as the basis of a motion picture. ABC negotiated with the songwriter's lawyer and thought they had a deal in spite of the fact that the lawyer representing the song wrote back numerous times to ABC stating that no such deal existed, as not all points had been resolved. The songwriter then entered into negotiations with Max Baer, who wanted to option the rights to the song for the same reason as ABC. Baer worked out a deal on all points. ABC tried to block the deal. The jury awarded Max Baer $2,000,000, holding ABC liable for tortuous interference with Max Baer's rights. One of the main points cited in the case is that a grant of rights may only be perfected by a signed agreement. For one, the copyright act requires that "a transfer of copyright ownership, other than by operation of law, is not valid unless an instrument of conveyance, or a note or memorandum of the transfer is in writing and signed by the owner of the rights conveyed or such owner's duly authorized agent." (17 U.S.C.§ 204 [a] [1976].) Correspondence between the songwriter's lawyer and ABC might have created a written agreement, but in this particular instance, the lawyer had insisted from the onset that a deal would not be closed until a contract was signed.

In short, if you insist on a signed contract in order for there to be a valid option or purchase of your material, you eliminate any persons who might claim they have a deal based on a proposal or correspondence that does not necessarily make clear the absence of an agreement. (Indeed, often agents or other representatives "close" a deal based on acceptance of material points, leaving to good faith negotiation other provisions. Sometimes you can rely on good faith to work out the rest of the details to your satisfaction. Sometimes, you cannot.) Insistence on a signed agreement eliminates the vagaries of closing a deal or saying you have reached an agreement if there are outstanding points that have not been resolved and you are concerned about them. It also eliminates the problem of an oral agreement. Even though copyright law requires a writing for a transfer to take place, if an oral agreement has been reached (a general rule of contract law is that oral agreements are binding), a claim may be made which may scare a studio away, unless the person making a claim agrees to walk away. The essential problem with an oral agreement is that until you prove that no such claim exists, a cloud may remain.

The *Max Baer* case is, indeed, a good lesson for would-be "cloud" creators. Hopefully, the size of the award will discourage many such persons. Because it is an unpublished decision, the case has no precedential value. But a court could very well make a similar ruling based on that kind of fact pattern.

Note that "clouds" are also created by persons claiming that a writer's material is similar to their own and insinuations of infringement. That is why producers are so paranoid about unsolicited submissions. Most producers will only accept submissions from known agents. Fortunately, these latter type of "clouds" are covered by errors and omissions insurance (see Chapter Three above) and thus are not as deadly to a project as the other examples I have pointed out in this chapter.

CHAPTER SIX

COLLABORATION AGREEMENTS

If you decide to write with someone else, you should work out an agreement with that person before you begin writing. That is, unless you don't mind the fact that your writing partner will effectively have rights equal to yours in connection with your joint work.

Any sophisticated buyer of collaborative material will require that all writers sign off on any agreement they may enter into. That means that if you want to option and/or sell the collaborative work to a third party, your collaborator will also have to agree not only as to the producer or studio that you want to be in business with, but also to the terms. In short, your partner can block a deal unless he/she is also satisfied with the terms.

The presumption with any joint work is that the collaborators are fifty-fifty owners of the finished product, unless otherwise specified. But suppose you wrote the story and your collaborator helped you with the script. You probably want additional compensation for your story, so you need to work that out. Another problem you might want to work out is the issue of rewrites. Is your partner tied to all rewrites that you might be asked to do? Suppose he/she is not available at the time. Will you be able to write without him or her? If you do all the rewriting yourself, will you be able to keep all of the compensation for the rewrite or will your partner expect a piece? Suppose you have a fight after the first draft. What happens if there are irreconcilable differences and you cannot work together? Can you proceed without your partner? As you can see, there are a number of problems that might arise.

To give you an idea of how complicated collaborations can be, I have reprinted below a deal which I made for a director/writer client who collaborated on a script with another writer.

SCREENWRITER'S COLLABORATION AGREEMENT

As of _____, 19____

Re: "_____"

AGREEMENT made at Los Angeles, California, by and between director/writer ("Director") and writer ("Writer") hereinafter sometimes referred to as collectively as the "Parties" and individually as "Party."

The Parties have written in collaboration a draft screenplay, hereinafter referred to as the "Work," based on a story idea and derived from previous drafts of screenplays by "_____," and are desirous of establishing all their rights and obligations in and to said Work.

NOW, THEREFORE, in consideration of the execution of this Agreement, and the undertakings of the Parties as hereinafter set forth, it is agreed as follows:

1. The Parties have collaborated in the writing of the Work and shall each own fifty percent (50%) of the actual revenues derived from the disposition of the Work itself, subject to the terms contained herein. Director agrees that she shall not

sell the Screenplay for less than $450,000_____. It is agreed that the sale price referred to in this paragraph for the Work shall not include revenues received for the story or any subsequent rewrites and drafts (unless otherwise negotiated pursuant to paragraph 9 below). It is further agreed that in the event Director dies prior to the disposition or sale of the Screenplay or prior to the time that any rights in the Screenplay would revert to Director, then at her death, all rights in the Screenplay shall revert to Writer subject to payment to Director's heirs of the same sums that would have been payable to Writer hereunder had Director not died and on the same basis as paid herein (i.e., 50% of the sums payable to Writer on a prospective basis). Director agrees that she will not employ a subsequent writer using her own funds.

2. Upon completion of the Work, it shall be registered with The Writers Guild of America, West, Inc., as a collaborative Work of the Parties. The copyright of the Work, however, shall be retained by Director only and shall be registered for copyright in the name of Director only. For said purposes and in connection therewith, Writer hereby assigns all of his right, title and interest in the Work to Director in perpetuity.

3. (a) Writer agrees that Director shall have the sole right to dispose of the Work and all underlying rights in connection therewith on terms to be negotiated by Director and her representatives in their sole discretion, subject to the following provisions:

(b) It is agreed by the Parties that the Work is intended 1) to be directed by Director at a salary no less than DGA minimum for such services and 2) that Director shall be the executive producer of said picture on terms to be negotiated in good faith by her, dependent on the budget of the picture. Both engagements shall be on a pay-or-play basis.

(c) Director agrees that Writer and his agent shall have the non-exclusive right after consultation with Director to (A) submit the Work to third parties and solicit offers to purchase the Work, which such offers must include a condition that the budget of the first picture produced based on the Work be no less than $13.5 million with an "A" list actor, the Work to be purchased for no less than $450,000, or (B) solicit offers to purchase the Work, which such offers must include conditions that, when the Picture is produced, Director shall be engaged to direct the Picture on a pay-or-play basis on terms to be negotiated in good faith by her provided she will receive a salary which is no less than DGA minimum for such services, and that she will executive-produce the picture on a pay-or-play basis on terms to be negotiated in good faith by him dependent on the budget of the picture. In the event such an offer is made, Director's agent and Writer's agent shall jointly negotiate the deal; provided that Writer agrees that Director shall have full authority to finalize any agreement. During this period, Writer agrees that she shall advise Director on a weekly basis of her progress with respect to the solicitation of offers and of any submissions to third parties or offers from third parties which have been made. Director shall also have the right during this period to offer the Work for sale and shall advise Writer on a weekly basis if he so requests of any submissions that he makes.

(d) If there shall be two or more agents negotiating jointly pursuant to this agreement, they shall be instructed to notify each other when they have begun negotiations for the sale or other disposition of the Work and of the terms hereof, and no agent shall conclude an agreement for the sale or other disposition of the Work by any of them, the matter shall immediately be referred to the Parties, but in the event of any disagreement, Director's decision shall be final with respect to any such negotiations.

4. Any contract for the sale or other disposition of the Work, where the Work has been completed by the Parties in accordance herewith, shall require, subject to the rules of the WGA, that the screenplay credit be given to the authors in the following manner:

Screenplay by Director and Writer
Story by Director

5. It is acknowledged and agreed that Writer's agent(s) shall not be entitled to commission any revenues payable to Director in connection with the Work. Similarly, the Director's agent(s) shall not be entitled to commission any revenues payable to Writer in connection with the Work.

The aggregate commission for the sale or other disposition of the Work shall be limited to ten percent (10%) and shall be divided among the respective agents in the same proportion that their respective client's shares bear to each other.

6. It is acknowledged that in connection with any contract entered into with a third party for the option or sale of the Work, that the negotiating Party(ies) shall endeavor to include a provision that Director's and Writer's expenses which have been or shall be incurred by either of them in connection with the writing, registration or sale or other disposition of the Work shall be reimbursed; provided that in no event will Writer be reimbursed for more than $2,500_____ .

7. All money or other things of value derived from the sale or other disposition of the Work shall be applied as follows:

(a) In payment of commissions, if any.

(b) In payment of any bona fide expenses or reimbursement of either Party for expenses paid in connection with the Work as set forth above.

(c) To the Parties in the proportion of their ownership.

8. It is understood and agreed that for the purposes of this Agreement, the Parties shall share hereunder, unless otherwise herein stated, the proceeds from the sale or any and all other disposition and exploitation of the Work and the rights and licenses therein and any elements thereof and with respect thereto, including but not limited to the following:

    a. Motion picture rights
    b. Sequel rights
    c. Remake rights
    d. Television film rights
    e. Television live rights
    f. Videocassette rights
    g. Merchandising
    h. Soundtrack
    i. Stage rights
    j. Radio rights
    k. Book and magazine publication rights

9. Should the Screenplay be sold or otherwise disposed of and, as an incident thereto, the third party financier agrees to pay Director for a paid revision of the Screenplay, then Director agrees that if at that time the Screenplay has not been sold, then she shall pay Writer 50% of the monies she receives for such rewrite after first applying the deductions delineated under paragraph 7(a) and 7(b) above, which sum shall be applicable against Writer's share of the Screenplay sales price pursuant to paragraph 1 above. Director agrees that she will consult with Writer regarding changes she will make to the Screenplay in such case.

Writer agrees that until a paid rewrite (pursuant to which Writer would receive WGA minimum as a team writer for said rewrite) is requested of Director, Director shall be entitled to rewrite the Screenplay herself and may consult with Writer regarding any changes of said material. After the first rewrite of the Work (which a third party has paid for) has been completed, Director shall have no further obligation to engage or pay Writer in connection with any subsequent rewrites.

10. If, prior to the completion of the paid rewrite, Writer shall voluntarily withdraw from the collaboration, the Director shall have the right to complete the rewrite alone or in conjunction with another collaborator or collaborators, and in such event the percentage of ownership with respect to all revenues, as provided herein, shall be revised by mutual agreement in writing (provided that in no event will Writer receive less than 30%), or, failing such agreement, by arbitration in accordance with the procedures hereinafter prescribed. Any withdrawal must be documented by written notice to the other Party. In the event Writer withdraws prior to commencement of the paid rewrite, then Director shall be entitled to retain all revenues in connection with said rewrite with no obligation to Writer.

11. Each Party represents and warrants to the other Party that he has not done and will not do any act which is inconsistent with or in conflict with this agreement or any of the rights of the Parties hereunder. Each Party represents and warrants to the other Party that all of their respective material is and shall be wholly original with the respective Party and will not violate or infringe upon any right of any third party including, without limitation, any copyright, right of privacy or publicity, or right to be free from libel or slander. Writer further represents and warrants to Director that he has neither exercised any of the rights in the Screenplay nor will do so except as set forth herein. Each Party shall defend, indemnify and hold harmless the other Party, their successors, licensees and assigns from and against all claims, liabilities, actions or cause of action, judgments, recoveries, damages, costs and expenses (including attorneys' fees) arising out of or in connection with any breach or alleged

breach of any of his representations, warranties, covenants or agreements herein or any use, exploitation or dissemination of his/her material.

12. Nothing contained herein shall be construed as obligating Director to use or exploit any results and/or proceeds of Writer's services hereunder, or to continue any use or exploitation if commenced.

13. In the case of a breach by Director of any of Director's obligations hereunder, Writer's sole right and remedy shall be an action at law for damages, and Writer specifically waives any right to injunctive or other equitable relief, to rescind this Agreement or any of the rights granted to Director hereunder or to terminate this Agreement.

14. Director shall have the unencumbered right to assign this Agreement, in whole or in part, to any third party, and all rights granted to Director hereunder and all representations, warranties and agreements made by Writer hereunder shall inure to the benefit of any such assignee of Director.

15. This Agreement shall be governed by, construed and enforced under the laws of the State of California, and suit may be brought in connection with this Agreement only in the State or Federal courts located in the State of California. If for any reason any provision of this Agreement is adjudged by a court to be unenforceable, such adjudication shall in no way affect any other provision of this Agreement or the validity or enforcement of the remainder of this Agreement, and the affected provision shall be modified or curtailed only to the extent necessary to bring it into compliance with applicable law. This Agreement expresses the entire understanding between Writer and Director, and supersedes any previous agreement, whether written or oral, between the Parties. This Agreement may be modified or amended only by a writing signed by the Party to be charged with said modification

or amendment. At Director's request, Writer shall execute a more formal long-form agreement reflecting such terms and the terms set forth in this Agreement, but until such time, if ever, as the Parties execute such an agreement this Agreement shall be binding. Writer also agrees to execute any documents which Director may reasonably require in order to confirm the Director the rights granted hereunder.

16. All notices, payments and correspondence that any Party hereto is required, or may desire, to serve upon any other Party hereto may be served by delivering same to the Party personally or by depositing the same in the United States mail, first class postage prepaid, or by sending the same, toll prepaid by telegraph or cable, addressed as follows:

If to Director:

_____

_____

_____

_____

With a concurrent copy to:

_____

_____

_____

_____

If to Writer:

_____

_____

_____

_____

or to such other addresses as the Parties may hereafter designate in writing. The date of such personal delivery, mailing or telegraphing shall be the date of the giving of such notice.

17. This Agreement shall be executed in sufficient number of copies so that one fully executed copy may be, and shall be, delivered to each Party and to the WGA. If any disputes shall arise concerning the interpretation or application of this Agreement, or the rights or liabilities of the Parties arising hereunder, such dispute shall be submitted to the WGA for arbitration in accordance with the arbitration procedures of the Guild, and the determination of the Guild's arbitration committee as to all such matters shall be conclusive and binding upon the Parties.

Very truly yours,

_____

Director

ACCEPTED AND AGREED:

_____

Writer

In the case of my director/writer client, from her point of view, she wanted to ensure that the project would be sold only if she was attached to direct her screenplay. My client also wanted the flexibility to make changes. If, after a certain period of time, the project could not be sold with her attached as director, then she was willing to step aside. This was fair for the other writer. He had put in the work. At some point, he wanted to know that he was going to be paid for it.

Her collaborator was also concerned that there be a minimum price for the script (as discussed above, it is wise to agree on this point up front). Also, in this particular contract, since the director had the right to hire subsequent writers and the salaries paid to any other writer(s) would ultimately reduce the collaborator's share, the collaborator wanted to protect himself by putting a ceiling on the reduction. Another issue which was resolved in this particular collaboration agreement was the order of credits.

This collaboration agreement also provides that in the event of a dispute, the writers will resolve their differences by arbitration. It is possible for you and your collaborator to bypass the court system. With an arbitration, you both choose one or three arbitrators (in Hollywood, retired judges can be hired for this purpose) and present your case. The arbitrator(s) will resolve the dispute, such as each writer's percentage of ownership in the script. If you are a WGA member, the WGA will arbitrate any disputes for you free of charge, even if only one writer is a member of the WGA, but keep in mind that you can always hire independent arbitrators even if you are not a member of the WGA. The cost is considerably less than going to court. These independent arbitrators will use procedures similar to those employed by the WGA. You and your partner agree to be bound by the decision. It works for both of you, so I encourage it. Courts are just too expensive for the average person. That is a sad reality of our legal system, so we all have to figure out a way around it.

This collaboration agreement also deals with the likelihood that there may be two agents involved (one for each writer) and ensures that no double commissions will be paid.

Of course, each collaboration agreement will have its own peculiarities. Read this agreement carefully. Should you decide to write a spec script with another writer, show the agreement to your partner and then address the relevant issues before you start writing. Even under the best of circumstances, disputes arise. Arguments are common in the creative environment. If you are going to devote your

valuable time to a writing endeavor, then you need to provide for a mechanism for dispute resolution. Put your
agreement down on paper, no matter how good a friend
your writing partner is. You will not regret it.

Here is an example of what can happen if you do not
work out your arrangement in advance:

I was approached by a young writer who had just graduated from college. He had written a first draft screenplay
and then met a producer. Together they worked on a final
draft without an agreement. The producer called himself
the writer's partner and took the position that since he
collaborated with the writer, he controlled the screenplay.
The writer asked me what his rights were and acknowledged the contribution that the producer had made to the
project. I asked him whether he had agreed on a price for
the script should a picture be made by the producer. He
told me he had not. As the writer had written the initial
screenplay and there was no agreement regarding that
screenplay (the one without any contribution from the
producer), I told him that I would call the producer and
try to work out a minimum price for his script. I proposed
a split of the revenues derived from any sale of the script
that was more favorable to the writer, since he had origi-
nated the project. I told the producer that it was also essential to work out an outside date for the producer to make
the picture, so that the writer would be able to proceed
without the producer at some point, if the producer could
not get the project off the ground.

The producer took the position that he had been involved with the project almost from its inception, that the
writer had contributed only an idea, not a story, that the
writer could do nothing without him, and he was unwilling
to set a price for the script (stating that the writer would

get a share of the profits). Further, the producer would not agree to a time limit.

The producer also took the position that unless the writer could prove that he had written his screenplay without any involvement from the producer (for instance, if the writer had registered his original screenplay with the Guild before meeting the producer, which he had not), the producer would call any other person that the writer tried to sell his screenplay to and tell him/her that the writer did not wholly control that screenplay and that a deal had to be made with the producer as well, effectively "clouding the chain of title" (see Chapter Five E above). I knew that we had to make a deal, the problem being that in cases such as these, until an independent determination is made (i.e., through a lawsuit, arbitration or settlement between the parties that may cost a lot of money), no one will touch the project.

The moral is: Straighten out your relationship with your partner before you begin working. The first thing you want to determine is how you can proceed if you and your partner do not agree at the time someone offers you a deal. One simple way to solve this is to say that neither writer will hold up a deal if a minimum agreed-upon price is offered for the screenplay. In other words, if you both agree that the screenplay is worth $200,000, and someone offers $200,000, then neither you nor your partner can *block* a deal. Second, if one person has contributed more and deserves more, work out exactly what the split will be in advance. As mentioned above, if you write the story, work out an agreed-upon value for that story either as a percentage of the whole purchase price (e.g., 20%) or a set price (e.g., $50,000). Agree upon the profit participation that you will accept (e.g., 5% of 100% of the net profits if you and your partner are awarded sole screenplay credit or 2 $\frac{1}{2}$% of 100% if you and your partner share screenplay credit with someone else). Agree on the floor for passive royalties (e.g., 50% for sequels, 33 $\frac{1}{3}$% for remakes—see discussion above). Agree that nothing out of the ordinary will be asked for on either side. Agree on a rewrite fee. Agree that one partner will be able to write without the other if one partner is unavailable, and agree on who, in that case, keeps the money for the rewrite. Keep in mind that the studio might insist on both partners writing, so the resolution of this issue might become problematic later on. Finally, discuss the issue of irreconcilable differences. If you originated the story and you have a fight with your partner, will you be able to proceed with rewrites without your partner, in which case, does your partner get a piece of the rewrite money?

The goal is to avoid *deadlocks* at all costs. And avoid surprises. Remember, the key benefit to having an agreement is to avoid ending up in a situation in which your collaborator, on hearing that someone is interested in your joint script, says, "I will not sell for less than one million and I also want to produce and direct it; otherwise, I am not selling." Believe me, it has happened in this town. True, even if you have an agreement, you cannot force your partner to put his/her signature on a piece of paper with a third party. But if you have an agreement with your partner that your partner will accept certain offers, at least you have the right to sue for damages if your partner does not agree to such terms when offered.

CHAPTER SEVEN

THE ROLE OF THE PRODUCER

A. HIS/HER RELATIONSHIP TO THE MATERIAL

I have added this chapter to the book because it is important for you to understand the continuing rights of the producer of your project to your material, and his function. Producers who work for studios are employees just like you. And unless a project gets made, they make much less than you. The average studio development fee for a producer of a feature film is $25,000. Producers often have agents: Keep in mind that it is a common practice for agents to commission the producer's salary, as well as the writer's compensation, when the agent delivers a piece of material to a producer who decides to take on that project. If you deduct the agent's commission plus legal fees, the producer is left with less than $20,000 to supervise the development of a script. One half of the $25,000 is paid on commencement of the writer's services for the studio, the other half is paid when the studio decides to make the picture or abandon it. That could take years. So producers who are not independently wealthy have to set up many projects just to make a living. As studios cut down on the number of pictures in development, survival becomes that much more difficult.

Producers (and on rare occasion, writers) are usually able to negotiate some sort of "progress to production clause" in their own contracts with the studios. In other words, the studios cannot just hold on to a piece of material forever if they do not do something with it. *Doing something* is defined rather generally. A typical clause looks like this: "Notwithstanding the foregoing, if for any consecutive six (6) month period there is no active development (e.g., all reading and writing periods have expired, there are no offers outstanding with respect to the writer, principal cast or director nor any budgeting or location surveying taking place), Producer may give studio notice and if studio fails to resume active development within ten (10) business days, the Picture shall be deemed abandoned."

Thus, the studio must actively either hire a writer, look for a writer, determine a budget, look for a star and the like. If, after notice, the studio fails to do something, then the project will be abandoned and it goes into turnaround to the producer.

Turnaround means that the studio gives the producer the right to take the project to another studio. If the producer does get another studio interested in the project, then the other studio must pay the first studio back its entire investment in the project (cost of writers, producer's development fee, messengers, producer's offices and the like), plus interest, plus a small piece of the net profits of the picture if it is made (generally 5%). The more money a studio spends on a project, the more difficult it is to get the project set up elsewhere.

Some studios have arrangements between themselves allowing the second studio to pay a fraction of the costs involved when the project is set up there and the balance if the picture is made. Note that the producer's turnaround agreement does not allow this and this is a side agreement between the studios. It is called a "reciprocal arrangement." Some studios, however, refuse to enter into these kinds of arrangements and insist on getting all their money back when the project is set up elsewhere. In other words, they will not wait until a picture is made to get all their money back. Either the second studio pays *all* costs when they get involved or they do not get the project.

Turnarounds are limited in time, generally for one year, sometimes eighteen months. If the producer with the turnaround rights does not set up the project at another studio within that period of time, the project remains with the studio which originally developed it and the producer may be *dismissed.* In short, for all of his endeavors, he collects his $25,000 development fee and has no further legal rights in the project (although many studios will keep the producer on notwithstanding the legal position). On the other hand, if he is lucky enough to set up the project elsewhere during the turnaround period, then he can try to negotiate with the second studio for another development fee. In most cases, the studio will argue that he has already been paid a development fee by the first studio (which fee the second studio must reimburse the first studio for) and is therefore *not* entitled to more money. However, if the producer is important enough, he might be able to eke out another $12,500 for several more years of work on the project. As you can see, it is not very much money.

On the other hand, if the project gets made, producers do hit the jackpot. Studio salaries for top producers can be $400,000 to $600,000 (in some cases $1,000,000 or more), depending on the producer. But remember, of all the projects developed, very few get made, so the odds are not good. As my partner, Peter Dekom, has said, "Being a producer is probably the worst job in Hollywood unless you are rich, a former studio head who makes a golden parachute deal with the studio after leaving, a manager/producer who can survive on the manager commissions or a writer/producer who can survive on his/her writing compensation." Being a plain old producer today is not a great way to make a living. Thus, producers today tend to be the ones who are truly passionate about filmmaking (they have to be passionate in order to survive) or those who spend their own money—and if it is their own money, they also have a stake in making sure the project gets off the ground.

Within the studio system, a strong producer can be a great asset to the young writer. For instance, if you are hired to write, he may ask you to let him read the script before you turn it in to the studio. He will probably make suggestions. He has been there before and he wants to make the best impression on the studio. Opinions are formed very quickly and if the first draft you turn in is not good, the odds of your staying with the project are greatly diminished. He will also help you fight your battles—as he has the relationship with the studio brass. It is important for you to build a strong bond with your producer and to get him in your corner. Simply put, he is in a better position to sway studio opinion and you should use him for that purpose. That is not to say that you should not fight your own battles. But it takes time to build relationships and when you are beginning, you will not have the long-standing relationship that the producer may have with the studio executive assigned to your project.

Of course, when you are starting out in Hollywood, it is hard to know who's who—more specifically, who can be trusted and who cannot. You want to get your script made into a picture. Someone finally expresses interest. You jump. Always remember that Hollywood is a "glamorous" industry (once you are in it, you will also realize it is very hard work). It attracts many individuals who want to add a little glamour to their lives. Thus, there are a lot of would-be producer types. Anyone can call themselves a producer. The real question is what they have produced and under what circumstances. You should be aware of what I call the "glue factor." Some people are producers because they have attached themselves, like glue, to a project and the only way to get the project made is to include them. They are like a nuisance suit. They are usually not the most respected producers in town.

Many young writers make mistakes. Here is an example. A young writer I know signed with a fledgling manager/producer. Believing that this person could be helpful to him, he agreed to sign a contract allowing this person to manage him for one year. The manager took a commission on all scripts sold or writing assignments obtained—not unusual. The manager also included a provision that he had the right to produce all projects which he set up. The problem with this provision is that he could technically block any deal if the studio/financier did not want to include him as a producer. Since this manager/"producer" had never produced, it was quite logical that the studio would consider him excess baggage, and indeed, in one such instance they did. That is when I was brought in. The writer wanted to try to make a deal with a studio/financier which had expressed interest in his project. The manager said that the writer could not make such a deal unless the studio/financier also agreed to let him be a producer. I called the manager and expressed my outrage. I also pointed out that he had a major conflict of interest —as a manager, he was supposed to promote his client's best interests. In his capacity as a "producer," he was not promoting those best interests, and he was effectively blocking any deal. He finally agreed that he would only ask for $50,000 and not take a commission. Because of the contract, there was a potential entanglement on the chain of title and my client agreed to try to get him $50,000, with the understanding that the producer could not block any deal if, at the end of the day, it turned out that the studio would break the deal over the producing salary. *Beware of would-be producers.*

If you want a career as a writer, you must remember that it is a business. As a businessman, you should find out everything about the person that you are going into business with. Ask questions. Find out the reputation of the producer. Do you know anyone who has worked with him, knows him, or of him? Do your research, and most importantly, avoid the sleaze factor in Hollywood, the wannabes who can only be someone by virtue of the "glue factor" and not by virtue of experience or talent.

Of course, even the most professional of producers will sometimes try to attach themselves as a producer to projects they do not own. This factor sometimes permeates even the highest levels of Hollywood. I was recently called by an agent friend who was trying to sell the motion picture and television rights to one of her client's books. She had sent the book to a well-known producer and asked the producer to make an offer. The producer did not. When the agent was on the brink of selling the book to someone else, news surfaced, the producer in question surfaced and told the agent it was her understanding that she had been given a free option. She also said that she would be a nuisance about it. While there were many legal loopholes in her argument (you need a written agreement to perfect chain of title and no purchase price had been established), the producer's stance did indeed create another level of complications. Since studios/financiers tend to protect producers who first pitch them projects, the producer who is in favor with the studio could very well arrange it so that the producer has to be taken care of before the studio will make a deal, notwithstanding the weak legal position. In other words, the studio could say, "That producer is attached or we do not make the deal." Believe me, it has happened. It is called "politics" and it exists in all businesses, most dramatically in Hollywood. This producer had strong relationships around town. Luckily, she backed off.

In short, you can never be sure that even the most experienced of producers will not try to pull something. Then again, if a strong producer is making waves, at least you know you have arrived, in a sense, and that your project is hot. In the end, if it is that hot, it will get set up with a major company and even has a chance to be made. The wannabe producers are in a different league and there is very little chance for an upside if there is a legal entanglement. Do your research. You have to if you want to survive.

B. YOUR RELATIONSHIP TO YOUR PRODUCER

I cannot emphasize enough the importance of relationships in Hollywood. Many contract disputes are settled because of relationships and not by lawsuits. It is important to build your relationships and keep them. Keep in mind that the studios have what they call "revolving doors." Today's executives may be out of work in a couple of years, only to surface again in more powerful position. There is a saying in Hollywood that executives fail upward. When studios are looking for new executives, they tend to pick persons who have been in that position before, regardless of their track records. What they are interested in are their *relationships.*

The same holds true for writers. Executives and producers like to pick writers who have strong relationships with them and with others. They want to know that you are not a troublemaker and that you are not on someone's secret blacklist. The stakes are high for studio executives. It is nice work if you can get it and they do not want to lose their jobs.

Times have been tough in Hollywood, as in the rest of the country. The writers with good relationships have survived. The ones who have not built strong relationships cannot find a job. I know several talented writers with substantial credits who cannot find jobs. They have no one to call. They do not fit in the studio mold. They are perceived as pushy and not pleasant to work with. Remember, if you have strong relationships, you can pick up the phone, independent of your agent. If you do not, you have to rely on your agent. And if you are cold at the studios, the agent cannot sell you. *Cold* meaning that no one wants to work with you again.

Producers and studios tend to work with people they like, with people who they perceive listen to their advice. If you have worked at a company and cannot get a job at that company again, you have obviously done something wrong and should ask yourself what it is and correct it before it happens again. Ideally, you will build one primary relationship with a major producer or company—become a "pet" writer. You want that level of relationship—to know that no matter how bad the times are, you can get some kind of writing assignment. It is a business and you must apply business principles to it as you would any other.

CHAPTER EIGHT

OTHER QUESTIONS YOU MAY WANT TO ASK YOUR AGENT OR LAWYER

This book is designed to give you an overview of the major issues that you will face in negotiating a writer's contract. Here is a list of some other issues that you may face during your negotiation. They are complicated issues; you should therefore talk to a lawyer or agent in respect of these areas. Unfortunately, I could probably write another book on these subjects alone, and thus am not able to discuss them in great detail. I want you to be aware of them in case they are of concern.

A. MATERIAL BASED ON FACT

If your screenplay is based on a true story and actual persons, you should consult a lawyer regarding releases that may be required from such persons. There are also numerous books on the law of defamation, rights of privacy and rights of publicity. Simply put, every individual has certain proprietary rights, and there are legal limitations concerning the exploitation of anyone's life in profitable ventures. Movies are intended to be profitable. Note that the law concerning depiction of actual persons in motion pictures is quite different from that pertaining to newspapers and other journalism, and you need to be very careful about exploiting any factual material.

Even if you claim that you have been truthful in your depiction, in writing a screenplay you will create certain scenes that you imagine might have taken place. You may or may not be accurate, so be careful. In addition, when depicting very personal facts, you need to be aware that each person has a right of privacy and you are not free to disclose certain personal aspects of anyone's life, even if you think such points are relevant to your story.

The studio will undoubtedly ask you for releases from the individuals whom you have depicted, and a thorough annotation of your screenplay, indicating where you got your facts from. Consult a lawyer first before you begin writing.

B. CONTRACTING ENTITY

Are you worried about the contracting entity? It may be a foreign corporation or a company that you've never heard of. There are a number of foreign corporations in Hollywood. Beware if you are asked to sign a contract with an offshore company. There are certain ways to guarantee jurisdiction in the United States and protect your compensation, but consult a lawyer to make sure you are protected.

If you are unsure about the financial stability of the corporation you are entering into a contract with, then you may want to ask for your money to be escrowed. Again, consult your lawyer.

C. SUBMISSION AGREEMENTS

As noted in this book, many producers will not accept material unless it is submitted by a known and reputable agent. Producers who are willing to accept the material without an agent involved will probably ask you to sign a submission agreement. They want to be assured that if they receive material from another source that is similar to yours, you will not sue by virtue of the similarity. Try first to find an agent or a lawyer to submit your material. If you can't, you will be forced to sign this customary submission agreement, but you may want to consult a lawyer before you do.

D. WRITING BASED ON OTHER SOURCE MATERIAL

If your work is based upon someone else's material, be sure that you can obtain the rights to the other material. Otherwise, your screenplay will be totally worthless. The producer cannot exploit a derivative work (a work based on other material) if he or she cannot obtain the rights to the underlying material. Again, consult your lawyer concerning the steps you need to take to ensure that you can obtain the rights.

E. TERMINATION RIGHTS

Producers customarily have certain rights to terminate your contract if you have breached, or are in default. This applies to option/purchase agreements and writing services agreements. There are also termination rights for disability if you are unable to perform services. The studio will need the right to terminate your services and get another writer. And if there is an industry-wide strike, or a force majeure event, and the development or production of the picture is delayed, again there may be certain other rights of suspension and termination. Consult your attorney regarding the terms that you can negotiate in respect of these termination provisions.

F. THE WRITERS GUILD BASIC AGREEMENT

Call the Writers Guild and get yourself a copy of this agreement. It will help you to understand the minimum rates and other protections that Writers Guild members are accorded. Ideally, you want to be accorded the same rights and privileges. This agreement will help you to understand the issues that face writers and the protections that the Guild has negotiated. The Writers Guild is a terrific organization that seeks constantly to assure that writers are protected in a world where writers are still considered totally disposable.

G. NEVER BE AFRAID TO ASK QUESTIONS

There is no question too annoying, too stupid or too complicated when it comes to your rights. You need to understand what your options are in order to prioritize your requests. And your requests should be realistic. Always remember that the best way to negotiate is to know what you can negotiate. You now have that knowledge. Use it well.

Acknowledgments

I would like to thank some of the people who have helped so generously in the preparation of this book:

CHARLOTTE SHEEDY, my agent, who inspired me to write this book. Her passion for books is unparalleled.

PETER DEKOM, my partner and teacher. His advice and encouragement, as always, were invaluable.

ELLEN GEIGER, who gave me the perfect title for this book and many wonderful ideas.

MARC GLICK, who gave generously of his time and sound advice.

RON PARKER for his many helpful suggestions.

CHRISTOPHER PHILLIPS, my good friend, who is always there.

PATRICIA BARRY, my godmother, for her steadfast and loving belief in me in all things.

BETSY BUNDSCHUH, my editor, for her special insight.

ELIZABETH STOULIL, my assistant, who graciously coordinated the entire process.

Many thanks also go to:

    Stephanie and Mark Agnew
    Howard Askenase
    Miranda Barry
    Philip Barry, Jr.
    Josette Bonte
    Leigh Brecheen
    Bobbie Edrick
    Earl Greenburg
    Judith Karfiol
    Jeffry Melnick
    Bruce Moccia
    Regula Noetzli
    Carol Vogel
    Richard Weiss

for their encouragement and patience.

To word processors Carl Tronco and Catherine Lydon
for their tremendous help.

INDEX

STEPHEN F. BREIMER graduated from Stanford University and from the UCLA School of Law. He is a member of the California bar and is currently a partner with the entertainment law firm of Bloom, Dekom, Hergott and Cook in Beverly Hills, California. While attending law school, he was a legal assistant for Chairman Mark Fowler at the Federal Communications Commission. Prior to law school he was a film producer, writer and story editor. He worked as associate producer of the television movies *Friendly Fire* and *First You Cry* and as producer and co-author of the feature film *Night Warning*, which was awarded Best Horror Film of 1982 by the Academy of Science Fiction, Fantasy and Horror Films. Stephen F. Breimer splits his time between the Hollywood Hills and Palm Springs. He is an avid collector of 1950s artifacts.